ISBN 978-1-5277-7657-9
PIBN 10890054

1 MONTH OF
FREE
READING

at

www.ForgottenBooks.com

By purchasing this book you are
eligible for one month membership to
ForgottenBooks.com, giving you
unlimited access to our entire
collection of over 1,000,000 titles via
our web site and mobile apps.

To claim your free month visit:

www.forgottenbooks.com/free890054

English
Français
Deutsche
Italiano
Español
Português

www.forgottenbooks.com

Mythology Photography **Fiction**
Fishing Christianity **Art** Cooking
Essays Buddhism Freemasonry
Medicine **Biology** Music **Ancient
Egypt** Evolution Carpentry Physics
Dance Geology **Mathematics** Fitness
Shakespeare **Folklore** Yoga Marketing
Confidence Immortality Biographies
Poetry **Psychology** Witchcraft
Electronics Chemistry History **Law**
Accounting **Philosophy** Anthropology
Alchemy Drama Quantum Mechanics
Atheism Sexual Health **Ancient History**
Entrepreneurship Languages Sport
Paleontology Needlework Islam
Metaphysics Investment Archaeology
Parenting Statistics Criminology
Motivational

CHARLES JACOBUS

Admitted to be the "Father of Roque;" one of America's most expert players, winning the Olympic Championship at St. Louis in 1904; an ardent supporter of the game and follows it minutely, and much of the success of roque is due to his untiring efforts; certainly there is no one better qualified to write on this subject than Mr. Jacobus.

DR. E. B. WARMAN

Well known as a physical training expert; was probably one of the first to enter the field and is the author of many books on the subject; lectures extensively each year all over the country.

W. J. CROMIE

Now with the University of Pennsylvania; was formerly a Y. M. C. A. physical director; a keen student of all gymnastic matters; the author of many books on subjects pertaining to physical training.

G. M. MARTIN

By profession a physical director of the Young Men's Christian Association; a close student of all things gymnastic, and games for the classes in the gymnasium or clubs.

PROF. SENAC

A leader in the fencing world; has maintained a fencing school in New York for years and developed a great many champions; understands the science of fencing thoroughly and the benefits to be derived therefrom.

SPALDING ATHLETIC LIBRARY

Giving the Titles of all Spalding Athletic Library Books now in print, grouped for ready reference

SPALDING OFFICIAL ANNUALS

No. 1 Spalding's Official Base Ball Guide
No. 1A Spalding's Official Base Ball Record
No. 2 Spalding's Official Foot Ball Guide
No. 2A Spalding's Official Soccer Foot Ball Guide
No. 3 Spalding's Official Cricket Guide
No. 4 Spalding's Official Lawn Tennis Annual
No. 5 Spalding's Official Golf Guide
No. 6 Spalding's Official Ice Hockey Guide
No. 7 Spalding's Official Basket Ball Guide
No. 8 Spalding's Official Bowling Guide
No. 9 Spalding's Official Indoor Base Ball Guide
No. 10 Spalding's Official Roller Polo Guide
No. 12 Spalding's Official Athletic Almanac

Group I.   Base Ball

No.   1 Spalding's Official Base Ball Guide.
No. 1A Official Base Ball Record.
No. 202 How to Play Base Ball.
No. 223 How to Bat.
No. 282 How to Run Bases.
No. 230 How to Pitch.
No. 229 How to Catch.
No. 225 How to Play First Base.
No. 226 How to Play Second Base.
No. 227 How to Play Third Base.
No. 228 How to Play Shortstop.
No. 224 How to Play the Outfield.
No. 231. {
  How to Organize a Base Ball Club. [League.
  How to Organize a Base Ball League
  How to Manage a Base Ball Club.
  How to Train a Base Ball Team
  How to Captain a Base Ball [Team
  How to Umpire a Game. [Team
  Technical Base Ball Terms.
}
No. 219 Ready Reckoner of Base Ball Percentages.

BASE BALL AUXILIARIES

No. 319 Minor League Base Ball Guide
No. 320 Official Book National League of Prof. Base Ball Clubs.
No. 321 Official Handbook National Playground Ball Assn.

Group II.   Foot Ball

No.   2 Spalding's Official Foot Ball Guide.
No. 334 Code of the Foot Ball Rules.
No. 324 How to Play Foot Ball.
No. 2A Spalding's Official Soccer Foot Ball Guide.
No. 286 How to Play Soccer.

FOOT BALL AUXILIARY

No. 332 Spalding's Official Canadian Foot Ball Guide.
No. 335 Spalding's Official Rugby Foot Ball Guide.

Group III.   Cricket

No. 3 Spalding's Official Cricket Guide.
No. 277 Cricket and How to Play It.

Group IV.   Lawn Tennis

No.   4 Spalding's Official Lawn Tennis Annual.
No. 157 How to Play Lawn Tennis.
No. 279 Strokes and Science of Lawn Tennis.

Group V.   Golf

No. 5 Spalding's Official Golf Guide.
No. 276 How to Play Golf.

Group VI.   Hockey

No.   6 Spalding's Official Ice Hockey Guide.
No. 304 How to Play Ice Hockey.
No. 154 Field Hockey.
No. 188 { Lawn Hockey.
         Parlor Hockey.
         Garden Hockey.
No. 180 Ring Hockey.

HOCKEY AUXILIARY

No. 256 Official Handbook Ontario Hockey Association.

Group VII.   Basket Ball

No.   7 Spalding's Official Basket Ball Guide.
No. 193 How to Play Basket Ball.
No. 318 Basket Ball Guide for Women.

BASKET BALL AUXILIARY

No. 323 Official Collegiate Basket Ball Handbook.

ANY OF THE ABOVE BOOKS MAILED POSTPAID UPON RECEIPT OF 10 CENTS

SPALDING ATHLETIC LIBRARY

Group VIII. Bowling
No. 8 *Spalding's Official Bowling Guide.*

Group IX. Indoor Base Ball
No. 9 *Spalding's Official Indoor Base Ball Guide.*

Group X. Polo
No. 10 *Spalding's Official Roller Polo Guide.*
No. 129 Water Polo.
No. 199 Equestrian Polo.

Group XI. Miscellaneous Games
No. 201 Lacrosse.
No. 322 Official Handbook U.S. Intercollegiate Lacrosse League.
No. 248 Archery.
No. 138 Croquet.
No. 271 Roque.
No. 194 { Racquets. Squash-Racquets. Court Tennis.
No. 13 Hand Ball.
No. 167 Quoits.
No. 170 Push Ball.
No. 14 Curling.
No. 207 Lawn Bowls.
No. 188 Lawn Games.
No. 189 Children's Games.

Group XII. Athletics
No. 12 *Spalding's Official Athletic Almanac.*
No. 27 College Athletics.
No. 182 All Around Athletics.
No. 156 Athletes' Guide.
No. 87 Athletic Primer.
No. 273 Olympic Games at Athens,1906
No. 252 How to Sprint.
No. 255 How to Run 100 Yards.
No. 174 Distance and Cross Country Running. [Thrower.
No. 259 How to Become a Weight
No. 55 Official Sporting Rules. [boys.
No. 246 Athletic Training for School-
No. 317 Marathon Running.
No. 331 Schoolyard Athletics.

ATHLETIC AUXILIARIES
No. 311 Amateur Athletic Union Official Handbook. [book.
No. 316 Intercollegiate Official Hand-
No. 302 Y. M. C. A. Official Handbook.
No. 313 Public Schools Athletic League Official Handbook.
No. 314 Public Schools Athletic League Official Handbook —Girls' Branch.
No. 308 Official Handbook New York Interscholastic Athletic Association.

Group XIII. Athletic Accomplishments
No. 177 How to Swim.
No. 296 Speed Swimming.
No. 128 How to Row.
No. 209 How to Become a Skater.
No. 178 How to Train for Bicycling.
No. 23 Canoeing.
No. 282 Roller Skating Guide.

Group XIV. Manly Sports
No. 18 Fencing. (By Breck.)
No. 162 Boxing.
No. 165 Fencing. (By Senac.)
No. 140 Wrestling.
No. 236 How to Wrestle.
No. 102 Ground Tumbling.
No. 233 Jiu Jitsu.
No. 166 How to Swing Indian Clubs.
No. 200 Dumb Bell Exercises.
No. 143 Indian Clubs and Dumb Bells.
No. 262 Medicine Ball Exercises.
No. 29 Pulley Weight Exercises.
No. 191 How to Punch the Bag.
No. 289 Tumbling for Amateurs.
No. 326 Professional Wrestling.

Group XV. Gymnastics
No. 104 Grading of Gymnastic Exercises. [Dumb Bell Drills.
No. 214 Graded Calisthenics and
No. 254 Barnjum Bar Bell Drill.
No. 158 Indoor and Outdoor Gymnastic Games.
No. 124 How to Become a Gymnast.
No. 287 Fancy Dumb Bell and Marching Drills. [Apparatus.
No. 327 Pyramid Building Without
No. 328 Exercises on the Parallel Bars.
No. 329 Pyramid Building with Wands, Chairs and Ladders
GYMNASTIC AUXILIARY
No. 333 Official Handbook I. C. A. A. Gymnasts of America.

Group XVI. Physical Culture
No. 161 Ten Minutes' Exercise for Busy Men. [giene.
No. 208 Physical Education and Hy-
No. 149 Scientific Physical Training and Care of the Body.
No. 142 Physical Training Simplified.
No. 185 Hints on Health.
No. 213 285 Health Answers.
No. 238 Muscle Building. [ning.
No. 234 School Tactics and Maze Run-
No. 261 Tensing Exercises. [nastics.
No. 285 Health by Muscular Gym-
No. 288 Indigestion Treated by Gym-
No. 290 Get Well; Keep Well.[nastics.
No. 325 Twenty-Minute Exercises.
No. 330 Physical Training for the School and Class Room.

ANY OF THE ABOVE BOOKS MAILED POSTPAID UPON RECEIPT OF 10 CENTS

SPALDING ATHLETIC LIBRARY

Group I.   Base Ball

No. 1—Spalding's Official Base Ball Guide.

 The leading Base Ball annual of the country, and the official authority of the game. Contains the official playing rules, with an explanatory index of the rules compiled by Mr. A. G. Spalding; pictures of all the teams in the National, American and minor leagues; reviews of the season; college Base Ball, and a great deal of interesting information. Price 10 cents.

No. 1A — Spalding's Official Base Ball Record.
Something new in Base Ball. Contains records of all kinds from the beginning of the National League and official averages of all professional organizations for past season. Illustrated with pictures of leading teams and players. Price 10 cents.

No. 202—How to Play Base Ball.
Edited by Tim Murnane. New and revised edition. Illustrated with pictures showing how all the various curves and drops are thrown and portraits of leading players. Price 10 cents.

No. 223—How to Bat.
There is no better way of becoming a proficient batter than by reading this book and practising the directions. Numerous illustrations. Price 10 cents.

No. 232—How to Run the Bases.
This book gives clear and concise directions for excelling as a base runner; tells when to run and when not to do so; how and when to slide; team work on the bases; in fact, every point of the game is thoroughly explained. Illustrated. Price 10 cents.

No. 230—How to Pitch.
A new, up-to-date book. Its contents are the practical teaching of men who have reached the top as pitchers, and who know how to impart a knowledge of their art. All the big leagues' pitchers are shown. Price 10 cents.

No. 229—How to Catch.
Every boy who has hopes of being a clever catcher should read how well-known players cover their position. Pictures of all the noted catchers in the big leagues. Price 10 cents.

No. 225—How to Play First Base.
Illustrated with pictures of all the prominent first basemen. Price 10 cents.

No. 226—How to Play Second Base.
The ideas of the best second basemen have been incorporated in this book for the especial benefit of boys who want to know the fine points of play at this point of the diamond. Price 10 cents.

No. 227—How to Play Third Base.
Third base is, in some respects, the most important of the infield. All the points explained. Price 10 cents.

No. 228—How to Play Shortstop.
Shortstop is one of the hardest positions on the infield to fill, and quick thought and quick action are necessary for a player who expects to make good as a shortstop. Illus. Price 10 cents.

No. 224—How to Play the Outfield.
An invaluable guide for the outfielder. Price 10 cents.

No. 231—How to Coach; How to Captain a Team; How to Manage a Team; How to Umpire; How to Organize a League; Technical Terms of Base Ball.
A useful guide. Price 10 cents.

No. 219—Ready Reckoner of Base Ball Percentages.
To supply a demand for a book which would show the percentage of clubs without recourse to the arduous work of figuring, the publishers had these tables compiled by an expert. Price 10 cents.

BASE BALL AUXILIARIES.

No. 319—Minor League Base Ball Guide.
The minors' own guide. Edited by President T. H. Murnane, of the New England League. Price 10 cents.

SPALDING ATHLETIC LIBRARY

No. 320—Official Handbook of the National League of Professional Base Ball Clubs.

Contains the Constitution, By-Laws, Official Rules, Averages, and schedule of the National League for the current year, together with list of club officers and reports of the annual meetings of the League. Price 10 cents.

No. 321—Official Handbook National Playground Ball Association.

This game is specially adapted for playgrounds, parks, etc., is spreading rapidly. The book contains a description of the game, rules and list of officers. Price 10 cents.

Group II. Foot Ball

No. 2—Spalding's Official Foot Ball Guide.

 Edited by Walter Camp. Contains the new rules, with diagram of field; All-America teams as selected by the leading authorities; reviews of the game from various sections of the country; scores; pictures. Price 10 cents.

No. 334—Code of the Foot Ball Rules.

This book is meant for the use of officials, to help them to refresh their memories before a game and to afford them a quick means of ascertaining a point during a game. It also gives a ready means of finding a rule in the Official Rule Book, and is of great help to a player in studying the Rules. Compiled by C. W. Short, Harvard, 1908. Price 10 cents.

No. 324—How to Play Foot Ball.

Edited by Walter Camp, of Yale. Everything that a beginner wants to know and many points that an expert will be glad to learn. Snapshots of leading teams and players in action, with comments by Walter Camp. Price 10 cents.

No. 2A—Spalding's Official Association Soccer Foot Ball Guide.

 A complete and up-to-date guide to the "Soccer" game in the United States, containing instructions for playing the game, official rules, and interesting news from all parts of the country. Illustrated. Price 10 cents.

No. 286—How to Play Soccer.

How each position should be played, written by the best player in England in his respective position, and illustrated with full-page photographs of players in action. Price 10 cents.

FOOT BALL AUXILIARIES.

No. 332—Spalding's Official Canadian Foot Ball Guide.

The official book of the game in Canada. Price 10 cents.

No. 335—Spalding's Official Rugby Foot Ball Guide.

Contains the official rules under which the game is played in England and by the California schools and colleges. Also instructions for playing the various positions on a team. Illustrated with action pictures of leading teams and players. Price 10 cents.

Group III. Cricket

No. 3—Spalding's Official Cricket Guide.

 The most complete year book of the game that has ever been published in America. Reports of special matches, official rules and pictures of all the leading teams. Price 10 cents.

No. 277—Cricket; and How to Play it.

By Prince Ranjitsinhji. The game described concisely and illustrated with full-page pictures posed especially for this book. Price 10 cents.

SPALDING ATHLETIC LIBRARY

Group IV. Lawn Tennis

No. 4—Spalding's Official Lawn Tennis Annual.

Contents include reports of all important tournaments; official ranking from 1885 to date; laws of lawn tennis; instructions for handicapping; decisions on doubtful points; management of tournaments; directory of clubs; laying out and keeping a court. Illustrated. Price 10 cents.

No. 157—How to Play Lawn Tennis.

A complete description of lawn tennis; a lesson for beginners and directions telling how to make the most important strokes. Illustrated. Price 10 cents.

No. 279—Strokes and Science of Lawn Tennis.

By P. A. Vaile, a leading authority on the game in Great Britain. Every stroke in the game is accurately illustrated and analyzed by the author. Price 10 cents.

Group V. Golf

No. 5—Spalding's Official Golf Guide.

Contains records of all important tournaments, articles on the game in various sections of the country, pictures of prominent players, official playing rules and general items of interest. Price 10 cents.

No. 276—How to Play Golf.

By James Braid and Harry Vardon, the world's two greatest players tell how they play the game, with numerous full-page pictures of them taken n the links. Price 10 cents.

Group VI. Hockey

No. 6—Spalding's Official Ice Hockey Guide.

The official year book of the game. Contains the official rules, pictures of leading teams and players, records, review of the season, reports from different sections of the United States and Canada. Price 10 cents.

No. 304—How to Play Ice Hockey.

Contains a description of the duties of each player. Illustrated. Price 10 cents.

No. 154—Field Hockey.

Prominent in the sports at Vassar, Smith, Wellesley, Bryn Mawr and other leading colleges. Price 10 cents.

No. 188—Lawn Hockey, Parlor Hockey, Garden Hockey.

Containing the rules for each game. Illustrated. Price 10 cents.

No. 180—Ring Hockey.

A new game for the gymnasium. Exciting as basket ball. Price 10 cents.

HOCKEY AUXILIARY.

No. 256—Official Handbook of the Ontario Hockey Association.

Contains the official rules of the Association, constitution, rules of competition, list of officers, and pictures of leading players. Price 10 cents.

Group VII. Basket Ball

No. 7—Spalding's Official Basket Ball Guide.

Edited by George T. Hepbron. Contains the revised official rules, decisions on disputed points, records of prominent teams, reports on the game from various parts of the country. Illustrated. Price 10 cents.

SPALDING ATHLETIC LIBRARY

No. 193—How to Play Basket Ball.

By G. T. Hepbron, editor of the Official Basket Ball Guide. Illustrated with scenes of action. Price 10 cents.

No. 318—Official Basket Ball Guide for Women.

Edited by Miss Senda Berenson, of Smith College. Contains the official playing rules and special articles on the game by prominent authorities. Illustrated. Price 10 cents.

BASKET BALL AUXILIARY.

No. 323—Collegiate Basket Ball Handbook.

The official publication of the Collegiate Basket Ball Association. Contains the official rules, records, All-America selections, reviews, and pictures. Edited by H. A. Fisher, of Columbia. Price 10 cents.

Group VIII. Bowling

No. 8—Spalding's Official Bowling Guide.

The contents include: diagrams of effective deliveries; hints to beginners: how to score; official rules; spares, how they are made; rules for cocked hat, quintet, cocked hat and feather, battle game, etc. Price 10 cents.

Group IX. Indoor Base Ball

No. 9—Spalding's Official Indoor Base Ball Guide.

America's national game is now vieing with other indoor games as a winter pastime. This book contains the playing rules, pictures of leading teams, and interesting articles on the game by leading authorities on the subject. Price 10 cents.

Group X. Polo

No. 10—Spalding's Official Roller Polo Guide.

Edited by J. C. Morse. A full description of the game; official rules, records; pictures of prominent players. Price 10 cents

No. 129—Water Polo.

The contents of this book treat of every detail, the individual work of the players, the practice of the team, how to throw the ball, with illustrations and many valuable hints. Price 10 cents.

No. 199—Equestrian Polo.

Compiled by H. L. Fitzpatrick of the New York Sun. Illustrated with portraits of leading players, and contains most useful information for polo players. Price 10 cents.

Group XI. Miscellaneous Games

No. 201—Lacrosse.

Every position is thoroughly explained in a most simple and concise manner, rendering it the best manual of the game ever published. Illustrated with numerous snapshots of important plays. Price 10 cents.

No. 322—Official Handbook U. S. Inter-Collegiate Lacrosse League.

Contains the constitution, by-laws, playing rules, list of officers and records of the association. Price 10 cents.

No. 271—Spalding's Official Roque Guide.

The official publication of the National Roque Association of America. Contains a description of the courts and their construction, diagrams, illustrations, rules and valuable information. Price 10 cents.

SPALDING ATHLETIC LIBRARY

No. 138—Spalding's Official Croquet Guide

Contains directions for playing, diagrams of important strokes, description of grounds, instructions for the beginner, terms used in the game, and the official playing rules. Price 10 cents.

No. 248—Archery.

A new and up-to-date book on this fascinating pastime. The several varieties of archery; instructions for shooting; how to select implements; how to score; and a great deal of interesting information. Illustrated. Price 10 cents.

No. 194—Racquets, Squash-Racquets and Court Tennis.

How to play each game is thoroughly explained, and all the difficult strokes shown by special photographs taken especially for this book. Contains the official rules for each game. Price 10 cents.

No. 167—Quoits.

Contains a description of the plays used by experts and the official rules. Illustrated. Price 10 cents.

No. 170—Push Ball.

This book contains the official rules and a sketch of the game; illustrated. Price 10 cents.

No. 13—How to Play Hand Ball.

By the world's champion, Michael Egan. Every play is thoroughly explained by text and diagram. Illustrated. Price 10 cents.

No. 14—Curling.

A short history of this famous Scottish pastime, with instructions for play, rules of the game, definitions of terms and diagrams of different shots. Price 10 cents.

No. 207—Bowling on the Green; or, Lawn Bowls.

How to construct a green; how to play the game, and the official rules of the Scottish Bowling Association. Illustrated. Price 10 cents.

No. 189—Children's Games.

These games are intended for use at recesses, and all but the team games have been adapted to large classes. Suitable for children from three to eight years, and include a great variety. Price 10 cents.

No. 188—Lawn Games.

Lawn Hockey, Garden Hockey, Hand Tennis, Tether Tennis; also Volley Ball, Parlor Hockey, Badminton, Basket Goal. Price 10 cents.

Group XII. Athletics

No. 12—Spalding's Official Athletic Almanac.

Compiled by J. E. Sullivan, President of the Amateur Athletic Union. The only annual publication now issued that contains a complete list of amateur best-on-records; intercollegiate, swimming, interscholastic, English, Irish, Scotch, Swedish, Continental, South African, Australasian; numerous photos of individual athletes and leading athletic teams. Price 10 cents.

No. 27—College Athletics.

M. C. Murphy, the well-known athletic trainer, now with Pennsylvania, the author of this book, has written it especially for the schoolboy and college man, but it is invaluable for the athlete who wishes to excel in any branch of athletic sport; profusely illustrated. Price 10 cents.

No. 182—All-Around Athletics.

Gives in full the method of scoring the All-Around Championship; how to train for the All-Around Championship. Illustrated. Price 10 cents.

No. 156—Athlete's Guide.

Full instructions for the beginner, telling how to sprint, hurdle, jump and throw weights, general hints on training; valuable advice to beginners and important A. A. U. rules and their explanations, while the pictures comprise many scenes of champions in action. Price 10 cents.

No. 273—The Olympic Games at Athens.

A complete account of the Olympic Games of 1906, at Athens, the greatest International Athletic Contest ever held. Compiled by J. E. Sullivan, Special United States Commissioner to the Olympic Games. Price 10 cents.

No. 87—Athletic Primer.

Edited by J. E. Sullivan, Ex-President of the Amateur Athletic Union. Tells how to organize an athletic club, how to conduct an athletic meeting, and gives rules for the government of athletic meetings; contents also include directions for laying out athletic grounds, and a very instructive article on training. Price 10 cents.

No. 252—How to Sprint.

Every athlete who aspires to be a sprinter can study this book to advantage. Price 10 cents.

No. 255—How to Run 100 Yards.

By J. W. Morton, the noted British champion. Many of Mr. Morton's methods of training are novel to American athletes, but his success is the best tribute to their worth. Illustrated. Price 10 cents.

No. 174—Distance and Cross-Country Running.

By George Orton, the famous University of Pennsylvania runner. The quarter, half, mile, the longer distances, and cross-country running and steeplechasing, with instructions for training; pictures of leading athletes in action, with comments by the editor. Price 10 cents.

No. 259—Weight Throwing.

Probably no other man in the world has had the varied and long experience of James S. Mitchel, the author, in the weight throwing department of athletics. The book gives valuable information not only for the novice, but for the expert as well. Price 10 cents

No. 246—Athletic Training for Schoolboys.

By Geo. W. Orton. Each event in the intercollegiate programme is treated of separately. Price 10 cents.

No. 55—Official Sporting Rules.

Contains rules not found in other publications for the government of many sports; rules for wrestling, shuffleboard, snowshoeing, professional racing, pigeon shooting, dog racing, pistol and revolver shooting, British water polo rules, Rugby foot ball rules. Price 10 cents.

ATHLETIC AUXILIARIES.

No. 311—Official Handbook of the A.A.U.

The A. A. U. is the governing body of athletes in the United States of America, and all games must be held under its rules, which are exclusively published in this handbook, and a copy should be in the hands of every athlete and every club officer in America. Price 10 cents.

No. 316—Official Intercollegiate A.A.A.A. Handbook.

Contains constitution, by-laws, and laws of athletics; records from 1876 to date. Price 10 cents.

No. 308—Official Handbook New York Interscholastic Athletic Association.

Contains the Association's records, constitution and by-laws and other information. Price 10 cents.

No. 302— Official Y.M.C.A. Handbook.

Contains the official rules governing all sports under the jurisdiction of the Y. M. C. A., official Y. M. C. A. scoring tables, pentathlon rules, pictures of leading Y. M. C. A. athletes. Price 10 cents.

No. 313—Official Handbook of the Public Schools Athletic League.

Edited by Dr. C. Ward Crampton, director of physical education in the Public Schools of Greater New York. Illustrated. Price 10 cents.

SPALDING ATHLETIC LIBRARY

No. 314—Official Handbook Girls' Branch of the Public Schools Athletic League.

The official publication. Contains: constitution and by-laws, list of officers, donors, founders, life and annual members, reports and illustrations. Price 10 cents.

No. 331—Schoolyard Athletics.

By J. E. Sullivan, Ex-President Amateur Athletic Union and member of Board of Education of Greater New York. An invaluable handbook for the teacher and the pupil. Gives a systematic plan for conducting school athletic contests and instructs how to prepare for the various events. Illustrated. Price 10 cents.

No. 317—Marathon Running.

A new and up-to-date book on this popular pastime. Contains pictures of the leading Marathon runners, methods of training, and best times made in various Marathon events. Price 10 cents.

Group XIII. Athletic Accomplishments

No. 177—How to Swim.

Will interest the expert as well as the novice; the illustrations were made from photographs especially posed, showing the swimmer in clear water; a valuable feature is the series of "land drill" exercises for the beginner. Price 10 cents.

No. 296—Speed Swimming.

By Champion C. M. Daniels of the New York Athletic Club team, holder of numerous American records, and the best swimmer in America qualified to write on the subject. Any boy should be able to increase his speed in the water after reading Champion Daniels' instructions on the subject. Price 10 cents.

No. 128—How to Row.

By E. J. Giannini, of the New York Athletic Club, one of America's most famous amateur oarsmen and champions. Shows how to hold the oars, the finish of the stroke and other valuable information. Price 10 cents.

No. 23—Canoeing.

Paddling, sailing, cruising and racing canoes and their uses; with hints on rig and management; the choice of a canoe; sailing canoes, racing regulations; canoeing and camping. Fully illustrated. Price 10 cents.

No. 209—How to Become a Skater.

Contains advice for beginners; how to become a figure skater, showing how to do all the different tricks of the best figure skaters. Pictures of prominent skaters and numerous diagrams. Price 10 cents.

No. 282—Official Roller Skating Guide.

Directions for becoming a fancy and trick roller skater, and rules for roller skating. Pictures of prominent trick skaters in action. Price 10 cents.

No. 178—How to Train for Bicycling.

Gives methods of the best riders when training for long or short distance races; hints on training. Revised and up-to-date in every particular. Price 10 cents.

Group XIV. Manly Sports

No. 140—Wrestling.

Catch-as-catch-can style. Seventy illustrations of the different holds, photographed especially and so described that anybody can with little effort learn every one. Price 10 cents.

No. 18—Fencing.

By Dr. Edward Breck, of Boston, editor of The Swordsman, a prominent amateur fencer. A book that has stood the test of time, and is universally acknowledged to be a standard work. Illustrated. Price 10 cents.

No. 162—Boxing Guide.

Contains over 70 pages of illustrations showing all the latest blows, posed especially for this book under the supervision of a well-known instructor of boxing, who makes a specialty of teaching and knows how to impart his knowledge. Price 10 cents.

No. 165—The Art of Fencing

By Regis and Louis Senac, of New York, famous instructors and leading authorities on the subject. Gives in detail how every move should be made. Price 10 cents.

No. 236—How to Wrestle.

The most complete and up-to-date book on wrestling ever published. Edited by F. R. Toombs, and devoted principally to special poses and illustrations by George Hackenschmidt, the "Russian Lion." Price 10 cents.

No. 102—Ground Tumbling.

Any boy, by reading this book and following the instructions, can become proficient. Price 10 cents.

No. 289—Tumbling for Amateurs.

Specially compiled for amateurs by Dr. James T. Gwathmey. Every variety of the pastime explained by text and pictures, over 100 different positions being shown. Price 10 cents.

No. 191—How to Punch the Bag.

The best treatise on bag punching that has ever been printed. Every variety of blow used in training is shown and explained, with a chapter on fancy bag punching by a well-known theatrical bag puncher. Price 10 cents,

No. 200—Dumb-Bells.

The best work on dumb-bells that has ever been offered. By Prof. G. Bojus, of New York. Contains 200 photographs. Should be in the hands of every teacher and pupil of physical culture, and is invaluable for home exercise. Price 10 cents.

No. 143—Indian Clubs and Dumb-Bells.

By America's amateur champion club swinger, J. H. Dougherty. It is clearly illustrated, by which any novice can become an expert. Price 10 cents.

No. 262—Medicine Ball Exercises.

A series of plain and practical exercises with the medicine ball, suitable for boys and girls, business and professional men, in and out of gymnasium. Price 10 cents.

No. 29—Pulley Weight Exercises.

By Dr. Henry S. Anderson, instructor in heavy gymnastics Yale gymnasium. In conjunction with a chest machine anyone with this book can become perfectly developed. Price 10 cents.

No. 233—Jiu Jitsu.

Each move thoroughly explained and illustrated with numerous full-page pictures of Messrs. A. Minami and K. Koyama, two of the most famous exponents of the art of Jiu Jitsu, who posed especially for this book. Price 10 cents.

No. 166—How to Swing Indian Clubs.

By Prof. E. B. Warman. By following the directions carefully anyone can become an expert. Price 10 cents.

No. 326—Professional Wrestling.

A book devoted to the catch-as-catch-can style; illustrated with half-tone pictures showing the different holds used by Frank Gotch, champion catch-as-catch-can wrestler of the world. Posed by Dr. Roller and Charles Postl. By Ed. W. Smith, Sporting Editor of the Chicago American. Price 10 cents.

Group XV. Gymnastics

No. 104—The Grading of Gymnastic Exercises.

By G. M. Martin. A book that should be in the hands of every physical director of the Y. M. C. A., school, club, college, etc. Price 10 cents.

SPALDING ATHLETIC LIBRARY

No. 214—Graded Calisthenics and Dumb-Bell Drills.

For years it has been the custom in most gymnasiums of memorizing a set drill, which was never varied. Consequently the beginner was given the same kind and amount as the older member. With a view to giving uniformity the present treatise is attempted. Price 10 cents.

No. 254—Barnjum Bar Bell Drill.

Edited by Dr. R. Tait McKenzie, Director Physical Training, University of Pennsylvania. Profusely illustrated. Price 10 cents.

No. 158—Indoor and Outdoor Gymnastic Games.

A book that will prove valuable to indoor and outdoor gymnasiums, schools, outings and gatherings where there are a number to be amused. Price 10 cents.

No. 124—How to Become a Gymnast.

By Robert Stoll, of the New York A. C., the American champion on the flying rings from 1885 to 1892. Any boy can easily become proficient with a little practice. Price 10 cents.

No. 287—Fancy Dumb Bell and Marching Drills.

All concede that games and recreative exercises during the adolescent period are preferable to set drills and monotonous movements. These drills, while designed primarily for boys, can be used successfully with girls and men and women. Profusely illustrated. Price 10 cents.

No. 327—Pyramid Building Without Apparatus.

By W. J. Cromie, Instructor of Gymnastics, University of Pennsylvania. With illustrations showing many different combinations. This book should be in the hands of all gymnasium instructors. Price 10 Cents.

No. 328—Exercises on the Parallel Bars.

By W. J. Cromie. Every gymnast should procure a copy of this book. Illustrated with cuts showing many novel exercises. Price 10 cents.

No. 329—Pyramid Building with Chairs, Wands and Ladders.

By W. J. Cromie. Illustrated with half-tone photographs showing many interesting combinations. Price 10 cents.

GYMNASTIC AUXILIARY.

No. 333—Official Handbook Inter-Collegiate Association Amateur Gymnasts of America.

Edited by P. R. Carpenter, Physical Director Amherst College. Contains pictures of leading teams and individual champions, official rules governing contests, records. Price 10 cents.

Group XVI. Physical Culture

No. 161—Ten Minutes' Exercise for Busy Men.

By Dr. Luther Halsey Gulick, Director of Physical Training in the New York Public Schools. A concise and complete course of physical education. Price 10 cents.

No. 208—Physical Education and Hygiene.

This is the fifth of the Physical Training series, by Prof. E. B. Warman (see Nos. 142, 149, 166, 185, 213, 261, 290.) Price 10 cents.

No. 149—The Care of the Body.

A book that all who value health should read and follow its instructions. By Prof. E. B. Warman, the well-known lecturer and authority on physical culture. Price 10 cents.

No. 142—Physical Training Simplified.

By Prof. E. B. Warman. A complete, thorough and practical book where the whole man is considered—brain and body. Price 10 cents.

SPALDING ATHLETIC LIBRARY

No. 185—Health Hints.

By Prof. E. B. Warman. Health influenced by insulation; health influenced by underwear; health influenced by color; exercise. Price 10 cents.

No. 213—285 Health Answers.

By Prof. E. B. Warman. Contents: ventilating a bedroom; ventilating a house; how to obtain pure air; bathing; salt water baths at home: a substitute for ice water; to cure insomnia, etc., etc. Price 10 cents.

No. 238—Muscle Building.

By Dr. L. H. Gulick. A complete treatise on the correct method of acquiring strength. Illustrated. Price 10 cents.

No. 234—School Tactics and Maze Running.

A series of drills for the use of schools. Edited by Dr. Luther Halsey Gulick. Price 10 cents.

No. 261—Tensing Exercises.

By Prof. E. B. Warman. The "Tensing" or "Resisting" system of muscular exercises is the most thorough, the most complete, the most satisfactory, and the most fascinating of systems. Price 10 cents.

No. 285—Health; by Muscular Gymnastics,

With hints on right living. By W. J. Cromie. If one will practice the exercises and observe the hints therein contained, he will be amply repaid for so doing. Price 10 cents.

No. 288—Indigestion Treated by Gymnastics

By W. J. Cromie. If the hints therein contained are observed and the exercises faithfully performed great relief will be experienced. Price 10 cents.

No. 290—Get Well; Keep Well.

By Prof. E. B. Warman, author of a number of books in the Spalding Athletic Library on physical training. Price 10 cents.

No. 325—Twenty Minute Exercises.

By Prof. E. B. Warman, with chapters on "How to Avoid Growing Old," and "Fasting; Its Objects and Benefits." Price 10 cents.

No. 330—Physical Training for the School and Class Room.

Edited by G. R. Borden, Physical Director of the Y. M. C. A., Easton, Pa. A book that is for practical work in the school room. Illustrated. Price 10 cents.

ARTHUR FARRELL.

SPALDING'S ATHLETIC LIBRARY
GROUP VI. - - No. 304

HOW TO PLAY ICE HOCKEY

BY
ARTHUR FARRELL

PUBLISHED BY THE
AMERICAN SPORTS PUBLISHING COMPANY
21 WARREN STREET, NEW YORK

GV8
.F2

PREFACE

Hockey! Fast, furious, brilliant, it is a most popular winter sport. Offspring of "Our Lady of the Snows," hockey is, among her many, varied games, the most fascinating, the most exciting, the most scientific. Canada no longer has a monopoly of the sport. The United States have the fever, and ice hockey is now a recognized winter sport where a few years ago it was unknown. Rinks are springing up everywhere, and even their greatest capacity cannot accommodate the enthusiastic attendances.

Hockey is a game for men; essentially it is a game for the youth. It needs strong, full-blooded men. Weaklings cannot survive in it, the puny cannot play it, and the timid have no place in it. It is, perhaps, the greatest game that man can play unaided. Hockey possesses all the spice of polo without the necessity for calling upon the animal kingdom.

ORIGIN OF HOCKEY

BY ARTHUR FARRELL

"How entrancing the sight ! what life is around !
The air is so bracing ! the snow on the ground !
The glimmering steel in its flash on the eye,
Marks out the line, as the skater goes by."

Webster's definition of hockey reads as follows: "A game in which two parties of players, armed with sticks or clubs, curved or hooked at the end, attempt to drive any small object (as a ball or a bit of wood) towards opposite goals."

The learned lexicographer must, of course, refer to the game of hockey as played in England, or to the game as played in Canada in the good old days when anything from a broom-handle to a shillalah was used as a hockey stick, and a tin can rendered service as a puck.

"O list, the mystic lore sublime,
The fairy tales of modern time."

To trace back the sport to its very birth is not within the province of this little work; besides, its earliest history seems lost in a background of Egyptian darkness.

In the development of hockey it is probable that hurling played an important part, and it seems quite likely that the present skilled game originated in a rough sport played at one time by the Romans. Joseph Strutt in 1801 described a game of hurley played by the Irish people in which a kind of bat was used, and this suggests a form of hockey played on the field. In Chambers's *Information for the People* it is stated that, "shinty in Scotland, hockey in England, and hurling in Ireland appear to be very much the same out-of-door sport." In an essay on the game an enthusiast writes that "the game existed in Ireland two thousand years ago, though possibly in a form that would not be recognized by the modern player, and its trail may be found here and there, across the story of social England from quite early days." The earliest use of the word occurs in certain local statutes enacted by the town of Galway in the year 1527, when, amongst prohibited games is named: "The horlinge of the litill balle with hockie stickes or staves." Hockey is described in Murray's *Dictionary* as equivalent to bandy or shinty. Shinty had a great vogue as an ice game and spread from the old world to the new with the pioneers. J. Ross Robertson, in the course of an article on the game, describes the habitants of French Canada playing a game of shinty on the ice. There is no doubt but that with the improvements in skates and the increased skill of men, the game improved bit by bit until the present skillful sport was reached.

The growth of hockey has been quick. It is a game of the present generation, and may truly be called a twentieth century pastime. Of mushroom growth, its development has been wonderful, but because it is a sport thoroughly American in spirit, it is well suited to the people of the northern part of this continent, and one well calculated to grow in popularity year by year. It is well within the memory of the present generation of sportsmen when the game first reached the dignity of receiving consideration from the grown-up folk. The first tour of Canadian teams in the United States was like the coming of an invading force. Now hockey is part of the winter season, coming with the first frost and lasting until it is time for the field sports to come in Spring. The sport has risen in jig time from a child's amusement to a college sport. New York and Montreal has its stirring battles, the metropolitan cities of two countries vieing with each other in interest in the game, and to such an extent that a season without an international contest would indeed be strange.

Hockey is a game requiring skill and courage, speed and strength, and the man in whom is centered these qualifications guided by a cool head is the man who will make the great player. No game in which man plays unaided has the speed of hockey. Roller polo is an approach, but the steel-shod hockey player is a veritable Mercury in comparison to his brother of the rollers.

To be a good hockey player a man must be master of his skates, for one thing. Then, he must be skilled in the use of his stick, adroit in avoiding collision, quick in judgment and possessed of an iron nerve that will not fail when in the face of impending danger. Hockey is dangerous, to this extent, that the unskilled player will receive many a hard knock, through collision and fall, which his more experienced and more skilled fellow will avoid. It requires fine experience to take a flier into the boards and escape unhurt, and it is wonderful to see a player go down amongst a group of men and escape skates and sticks by scant inches. How this may be done is not a matter to be told of in books, it can only be learned by hard and stern experience. Some men, many in the States, have taken up hockey in mature years, but the generality of Canadian players are chaps who have grown up, stick in hand, as it were, fellows who have learned their skating and stick-handling from early boyhood. In Canada they play the game in the schools, so that it is quite understandable how they become proficient players.

Of all the games that developed from the old Roman sport the British hockey alone shaped the destiny of ours. There can be but little doubt but that "shinny," the forerunner of our scientific hockey, is the interpretation of the game as played on this side of the water, adapted in its application to the climate of the country. Hockey in England is played in the winter on the frozen ground. It consists in driving a ball from one point to another by means of a hooked stick. The players are divided into two teams, each of which has its goals, which are fixed towards either end of a tolerably spacious ground. The goals are two upright posts, about six feet apart, with a cross pole placed at the height of four feet. Through these the ball must be driven in order to score a point. As regards the playing of the game, it is unnecessary further to speak, because it bears but little reference to hockey as played in Canada and the United States. Suffice it to say that in the shape of the sticks, not limited in their proportions, in the nature of the object that was used as a ball, in the unlimited number of the players and in its principles, it is the parent of "shinny on the ice."

Shinny, so called, perhaps, on account of the frequent danger to which a player's shins were exposed, was a grand, exhilarating sport. It had a hold upon us that the chilly atmosphere, or "the love we bore for learning," could not unfasten. Boys swarmed to the lakes in battalions and rattled along on old iron or wooden skates tied to their feet with rope. A few broken bones, a few frozen fingers, but, never mind, there were plenty of men to replace the dead. What a sight did a shinny match present! Hundreds on the same sheet of glare black ice, all eagerly engaged in one glorious game. What laughing, calling, cheering and chasing there was to be sure! With their bright eyes and rosy cheeks they dart now in one direction, now in another, till the great congealed bay roars and cracks with its living weight. The ball is in all directions in seconds of time, till finally the vast struggling crowd surges toward the goals, surrounds them, and a fierce, lucky swipe knocks it through, while a hundred lusty voices cry their loudest: "Game! Game!"

Like the fabled Greek who used to give his time so undividedly to his work that he forgot his meals, these enthusiasts of an infant game forgot their meals, forgot their schools, forgot everything save the game itself, but when darkness came on and their shadows grew longer, they returned home, with fresh air in their expanded lungs, strength in their limbs, and with a keen, bright eye, "seeking what they might devour."

As time wore on, the gradual development of rules and regulations wrought, in this warlike pastime, the important changes that were, in time, to give birth to the science that characterizes hockey as the peer of clean, exciting, fascinating games.

Half a dozen years ago the game was practically Canadian. Now in its development it belongs to America and it seems that the time is coming when the younger generation of boys in the northern states will have developed the talent needed to meet the Canadians on equal grounds. Now it cannot be said that they are able to do this at the moment. Canadians are freely scattered among the teams, while in the International professional league it would be an Augean task to throw a stone without hitting a Canuck. But, because the younger generation, the schools and the colleges, are taking a keen interest in the game, this state of affairs will not continue for long, and soon indeed it will be that the growing American boy will be able to go after his Canadian rival with a skill born, not developed. It speaks well for the spirit of the American that he has been able to do so well against his better qualified Canadian rival; it speaks volumes for the future.

In Canada hockey is a national winter game. It is played on the Atlantic coast, and three thousand miles due west the game has a hold on the hearts of the people possible only in a country of deep enthusiasms. Wherever there are enough people residing together to form a good sized village, there is a hockey club to be formed. The big cities have local leagues, and inter-city hockey is an ordinary matter in the winter months. But the highest development of hockey has been in the interior, and in seeking to give honor to those responsible for the present high form of the game, laurels must be divided between the cities of the middle east and those of the middle west. In the east these will be Montreal, Ottawa, and Quebec; in the west, Winnipeg and Kenora, formerly known as Rat Portage. The one large city in between these two groups is Toronto, but this progressive city has not yet been able to produce the same skilled aggrega- tions which have fought the battles of east and west. This is probably due to climatic conditions. Toronto does not have the same steady winter weather which will be found in Montreal and in Winnipeg. Therefore there is not the same opportunity for practice, hence there cannot be the same skill. Toronto's way to reach the same eminent position would be to build an artificial ice plant. Montreal, Quebec, and Ottawa have ice from middle December to middle March. In the west, particularly in the province of Manitoba, there is ice at the end of November and it usually remains until middle March. In the cities men- tioned, hockey obtains to the same relative position as base ball does in summer in the United States. The games are followed with a great deal of enthusiasm and crowds at matches between first class teams are limited only by the accommodation of the rink buildings. The games are played at night and in covered buildings, and as an ice surface approximating 15,000 square feet must first be provided, it will be seen that very large buildings are required for the purpose. The Auditorium in Winnipeg and the Arena in Montreal are the largest hockey rinks in Canada. The Arena in Montreal is a building of steel, brick, and wood. The ice surface is 80 feet in width by 200 in length. The seating capacity is 6,000 and the crowding capacity is twenty-five per cent. additional. The building is arena shaped and is almost ideal for the purpose of hockey players. The Auditorium in Winnipeg has about the same ice surface and its general features are those of the Arena.

A list of leagues in Canada would require a volume in itself. However, the chief leagues are confined to a handful. There are two good leagues in the Maritime Provinces and several minor leagues occupy territory before Quebec is reached. The Eastern Canada Hockey League is the most important body in Canada, not because of its size, but because of the quality of game played by its members. This league is interprovincial in character. There are six clubs forming the membership and they represent three cities, Montreal, Ottawa, and Quebec. The clubs are: Victoria, Montreal, Shamrock, and Wanderer, of Montreal; Ottawa, of Ottawa; Quebec, of Quebec. The league has existed under various names since the beginning of organized hockey. Formerly it was known as the Amateur Hockey Association of Canada. This organization was disrupted and the Canadian Amateur Hockey League followed. In turn that gave way to the Eastern Canada Amateur Hockey League, which, in turn, made way for the present organization. Sporting politics have been responsible for all these changes. Originally the association was made up of Senior and Intermediate clubs. The latter grew so strong as to hold the balance of power and when this happened the senior clubs broke away and formed a close corporation, as strong in its own way as the National Base Ball organization. After that membership changed whenever policy dictated it. There does exist in the middle east a proud association known as the Junior Hockey Association of Canada. This organization is limited to junior clubs and has been in continuous existence for over twenty years, a record to be proud of.

Hockey in the neighboring province is under the sway of the Ontario Hockey Association. This is the largest hockey organization in Canada, numbering its clubs by the hundreds and its individual members by the thousands. For the purposes of this organization the province is divided into districts, and the game is divided into three grades, senior, intermediate and junior. The management of the organization is capable and it is doing fine work for the sport in Ontario.

Further west there is a big league which includes clubs in Winnipeg, Kenora, and Brandon, and here hockey assumes its highest development west of Toronto. Between this league, under various forms, and the middle east some great battles have taken place, and a meeting of the east and the west is always a memorable occasion.

To the McGill College and Victoria hockey teams of Montreal the game of hockey owes its present state. These two were the first regularly organized hockey clubs in the world, the former preceding the latter by a very short time. Previous to the formation of the above organizations about 1881, teams existed in Montreal and Quebec, but the only rule that was well defined was the one which demanded that every man should "shinny on his own side." Do what you might, play on what you liked or with what you liked—and as long as you shinnied on your own side you were within the law.

All kinds of sticks were used, long knotted roots, broom handles, clubs, and all kinds of skates were employed, from long, dangerous reachers to short, wooden rockers. On each particular occasion the captains agreed, before the game, upon the rules that they would abide by or disregard, so that the rules that governed one match might be null and void for another. The puck was a square block of wood, about two cubic inches in size, on which a later improvement was the bung of a barrel, tightly tied round with cord. Body checking was prohibited. so was lifting the puck; if the puck went behind the goal line it had to be faced; the referee kept time and decided the games; the goal posts, placed, at times, like ours, facing one another, were also fastened in the ice in a row, facing the sides, so that a game might be scored from either road, the forward shooting in the direction of the side of the rink, instead of toward the end, as we do.

As soon as the Montreal Victorias were organized, the secretary of that club wrote to every city in Canada for information regarding the rules of hockey, but the result was unsatisfactory, because he could get none. When, shortly after, the Crystals and M. A. A. A. had formed teams, and the Ottawas and Quebecs had come into existence, the first successful matches, played under a code of rules that had been drawn up and accepted, were brought about by the challenge system. The first series of games took place during the first winter carnival, in 1884, and was played on the cold river rink, and the second during the second carnival, in the Victoria rink, "when," as history relates, "the players were slightly interfered with by the erection of a large ice-grotto in the rink."

In 1887 the challenge system was done away with, and the Victorias, Crystals, Montrealers, Quebecs and Ottawas formed the Amateur Hockey Association of Canada, which, in the good effects that it has produced, constitutes the second epoch in the history of the game, because from this date hockey made rapid strides in its advancement as a popular, scientific sport.

The game was first introduced into the United States some years ago by a Montrealer, Mr. C. Shearer, who was studying in the Johns Hopkins University, Baltimore.

He formed a team among the students of that institution, and was successful in inducing the Quebec team, which was the first Canadian seven to play across the border, to travel to the Oriole city for a series of games. In 1895 the Shamrocks and Montrealers, of Montreal, delighted audiences in New York, Washington and Baltimore. Since that time the Queen's College team has played in Pittsburg, and nearly all of Canada's leading clubs have sent their representatives to play in the different American rinks.

The game in the United States now made rapid strides. Colleges and schools took an interest in the game and organized teams, schedules were drawn up, the public flocked to the rinks to see the games, and now it is a most popular winter sport.

Artificial rinks are found in the principal cities of the country, and afford to players a great advantage, as there is never a scarcity of ice. They are opened in the autumn and remain open for skating until spring; besides, being comparatively warm, spectators are not kept away from them, however inclement the weather may be. A short time ago almost any Canadian team could defeat, with comparative ease, the best seven that could be found in the United States. But now a different complexion colors the comparison between the clubs, because several teams have arrived at such a high degree of science in the game, that the excellence of their playing makes them eligible to honorably compete with the peers of the game in Canada. Indeed, it seems that the day is not far distant when the holders of the highest honors in hockey matters will have to look to themselves if they wish to successfully defend their laurels against a worthy opponent.

Hockey was first played in Europe by another Montrealer, Mr. George A. Meagher, world's champion figure skater, and author of "Lessons in Skating."

In Paris the first European team was formed, and the gay Parisians took most enthusiastically to it. London boasted of the second club in Europe, and in less than one season more than five teams chased the rubber disc in that city.

Scotland was the next country to enjoy the game. In the artificial ice palace, Sauchiehall street, Glasgow, the first practices were held, and so proficient did the canny Scotchmen become that a game with the team of the Palais de Glace in Paris was arranged. A series of six matches was played in one week with the French team, and the crowds that witnessed the games fairly raised the roof with their clamorous applause. The "Figaro," the leading newspaper in France, described hockey as a game that promised to excel all other sports in Paris in point of popularity and "scientific possibilities."

THE SCIENCE OF THE GAME

What is the objective point, the central idea, in the game of hockey? To score—to lift, slide, push or knock the puck through your opponents' goals.

A team, and each individual member of a team, should concentrate every idea, every thought on this one desire, and each play, each move should point to it, as the rays of the sun are converged through a glass to the focus.

That play is vain which does not tend to bring a team, or a member of a team, to a position from which the desired point can be gained—a useless move effects the position of a team, throws the players out of poise.

The fancy play, the grand-stand play, is a waste of energy, childish, worthless. The play that counts, the play that shows the science of the man who makes it, is the immediate execution, in the simplest manner, of the plan that a player conceives when he considers the object of his playing. In other (geometrical) words the shortest distance between two points is a straight line, and applied to the science of hockey, it means that a player should take the shortest and quickest way of obtaining the desired effect, which, by analysis, is oftentimes the most scientific.

When it is said that every player of a team should strain nerve and muscle to score a goal, the meaning is not that each individual member should strive to do the act himself, but that he should use every effort to assist him to score who is in the most advantageous position to do so. The selfish desire on the part of even one man to make the point oftentimes entails the loss of a match.

Although by nearing his opponents' defence with the puck a player naturally approaches the position from which to shoot, he will invariably confuse his adversaries more successfully, and often secure for himself or his partner a much more desirable vantage ground, by

FACING OFF AT BEGINNING OF PLAY.

passing the puck to the latter before reaching the cover-point. Indeed, if the question of praise be mentioned, there is often more due to the player who assists by a clever bit of combination work than to the man who scores the game.

The secret of a team's success is combination play, in other words, unselfishness. It means the giving of the puck to a player of one's own side who is in a better position to use it than the man who first secures the rubber. It is the science of mutual help. As in lacrosse and foot ball, it is a "sine qua non." The team that indulges most in this scientific play has the less hard work to do and is necessarily the freshest when the trying end of the match comes round, because combination play minimizes the work in this arduous game.

As soon as a player secures the puck he should first look for an opening and then size up, at a glance, the position of his confreres. It is, indeed, a question whether it be not more scientific, more successful to first look for a good opportunity to pass the puck to a partner, and then, if none such presents itself, to force a clearing.

It happens that a fast forward can, by his own personal efforts, score one, two or perhaps three goals, but toward the close of the game he is no longer able to do effective work, because his selfish exertions have played him out, and when necessity demands that, because of poor assistance from his partners, a good man should indulge in individual work, such may be permissible, but the team thus handicapped cannot expect to win from a well-balanced aggregation.

Combination in hockey is the scientific means to the end at which the players aim, viz., the placing of a man of the team that makes the play in the best obtainable position to shoot a goal, and should be carried on only until that position is attained.

It is possible to indulge even too much in combination work, necessary as it is on most occasions, and thus the virtue may be turned into a vice. It should not be played too freely by men in front of their own goals, and as it is merely a means to an end, an over indulgence in it is a loss of time, of which hockey is too fast a game to allow.

In close quarters the puck should be passed to a man's stick, and not in a line with his skates. A scientific player, rushing down the ice with a partner, will give the puck to the latter, not in a direct

DEFENCE OF THE GOAL—Stopping the puck with the hockey stick.

line with him, unless they are very close together, but to a point somewhat in advance, so that he will have to skate up to get it. The advantage in this style of passing is that the man who is to receive the rubber will not have to wait for it, but may skate on at the same rate of speed at which he was going before the puck was crossed and proceed in his course without loss of time.

The puck should be passed in such a manner that it will slide along the ice and not "lift," because it is difficult to stop and secure the rubber when it comes flying through the air. There are times, of course, when a "lifted" pass is necessary; for instance, when the line on the ice between the passer and the receiver is obstructed, but otherwise the "sliding" pass is advisable.

When two "wing" men play combination together in an attack, the puck should scarcely ever be passed directly to each other, but should be aimed at the cushioned side of the rink, some distance in advance of the man, so that he may secure it on the rebound. The rink is so wide that it is difficult to pass the puck accurately from one side to the other, especially during a rush, so the above means is recommended.

When three or four forwards are making a rush, the puck should be held by one of the centre players until the cover-point is reached, because in such a play the latter does not know to which man the rubber is to be passed, for it may be given to the right or the left wing or even to the other centre player, but when, in an attack, a wing man has the puck, the cover-point knows that he must necessarily cross it out to the centre and is prepared for the play.

When the forwards of a team are operating around their opponents' goals and cannot get an opening, it is sometimes advisable for them to slide the puck to their cover-point if he is well advanced towards the middle of the rink, because this will probably coax out the defence, and the change of positions may create the desired effect.

One of the most successful, and, perhaps, the most neglected of combination plays is the following: when a player secures the puck behind or to the side of his opponents' goals, he should, if he has time, slide it to his assistant who is in the best position to receive it, or, if not, to the side where he knows that one of his men, by a preconcerted, practiced arrangement, awaits it, but he should never send

DEFENCE OF THE GOAL—Stopping the puck with the leg.

it, with a blind, trust-to-luck shot directly in front of the goals, because the point and cover-point should be, and usually are, stationed there. This simple play is often attended with great success. To guard against this play the defence men and forwards of the attacked goals should see that, when the puck is around the goal line, each of their opposing forwards is carefully checked.

Each player should be careful to remain in his own position, and in order to acquire the habit of so doing, every man should make it a point in each practice, however unimportant, to cling to the particular position on the team which he is intended to fill. It is a grievous mistake for a wing man to leave his position and play in the centre of the ice or on the side to which he does not belong, or for a centre player or rover to wander to the wings, because as each man has a cover, a check, on whom, in turn he should bestow his attention, he gives his opponent, when he leaves his place, an opening that the latter should not, and would not have if he were properly watched, besides, the forwards and the defence men of an experienced team ought to be able to know where their assistants are or, rather, should be by judging from their own positions. When a man strays from his own territory, a brilliant combination play may easily be lost through his absence from his proper place.

Each player of a team should occupy his position so unfailingly in practice, and the team should indulge in combination work to such an extent, that, in a match, a forward ought, at times, to be able to slide the puck to an assistant without even having to look to know where the latter is. If perfection be aimed at, and it should, the point of following up should be so regular, so systematic that this play may be successfully indulged in, because, with every man working in his position, like so many movements in a clock, a forward with the puck, in advance, should know without looking, where each of his partners follows.

The prettiest spectacle afforded by a good hockey match, is the rush down the ice, four abreast, of the forwards. This play to a man of sporting instincts, verges on the beautiful.

When four men in a line, racing at lightning speed, approach the defence of their opponents, it is then that the goal-keeper of the attacked party sees danger signals floating in the air, because the

WRONG WAY TO HANDLE STICK—Using one hand instead of two.

assistance he will receive from his defence men, is, on these occasions, problematical. If they crowd in upon him, his view of the play is obstructed ; if the cover rushes out he may not use the body-check, because he does not know which man will have the puck, and therefore cannot afford to waste time and energy on one who has already passed the rubber, or who will do so, and the point man must necessarily keep his position unless some fumbling occurs. But should the forward line advance four abreast ? , This is a serious question.

When such a rush is being made, one slip, one fumble, a fraction of a second lost, will throw at least three of the forwards off-side, out of play. It is a good deal safer and more satisfactory for one man, say the rover, to follow the three other forwards, slightly in the rear, so that if such a slip, such a fumble occurs, he will be close on hand to recover the puck, and quickly place his men in play.

More than two forwards should never be behind their opponents' goals at the same time, because it is necessary that some should be in front, in case the puck should be passed out to them, and, moreover, if it be lifted down by their adversaries, they have a chance of stopping it in a good position to shoot for the goals.

At least two men should be in front, in order to follow up any attack that their opponents might make on their goals. It is surprising how much trouble can be caused a forward line by a persistent forward who nags at them from behind. He can often break up a combination, and create more confusion among them than a defence man, because they know what to expect from the latter and are on the lookout for him, but find it difficult to deal with a fast man who bothers them in this way. It is in this work that a fast skater shows to advantage.

Should a forward who has gone down the ice alone attempt to pass the cover-point and point of the opposing team, before shooting? Yes and no. If the cover-point is well up towards the middle of the rink and the point is not too near the goals, let him strain every nerve and muscle to dodge them both and then shoot, but if the defence men are bunched in front of the poles, he should lift without trying to pass the cover-point. His shot, in this case, will often prove effective, because, having his two assistants directly in front of him, obstructing his view of the play, the goal keeper cannot easily stop a

DEFENCE OF THE GOAL—Stopping the puck with the skate.

low, hard, well directed "puck," besides, he will deprive the cover-point of the pleasure of "using his body."

On approaching the cover-point, a forward, before passing the puck, should incline a good deal towards the opposite side to which he is going to send it, because in so doing he will force the cover-point to leave his place, and thereby create a better clearing for action.

It is a peculiar fact that defence men, in their positions, are usually less apt than forwards to get excited, which might be accounted for by this that it is a great deal easier for them to prevent a man from scoring than it is for him to score, and, besides, they are in their own territory moving at comparative ease, whilst the rushing forward tears down at full speed and has time enough only to think of how he may pass the puck or how elude the cover-point. The forward player has more to think of, more to do in order to score, than the defence men have in preventing him.

It is in the attack on goals that a forward's coolness will assist him. For a man to know what to do, when he is near his opponents' defence, requires thought. The ever-varying changes in conditions and positions prevents a man from having any set line of action in an attack. Every rush is confronted by a different combination of circumstances, and a forward must know, on each separate occasion, the play that is best calculated to effect the desired result. This knowledge is the attribute of an experienced player and must go hand in hand with coolness. Practice teaches a man what to do, coolness enables him to do it.

It is singular, but remarkably true, that a forward who could not win even a "green" skating race, can excel as a lightning hockey player. It is one of the ingenious paradoxes of the game, that cannot be explained. A man who can beat another in a race is not necessarily a faster forward than that man. Examples on every team prove the contention. Perhaps the possession of the puck, the excitement of the game, the attraction that an assistant has when skating near him, gives to the man who may not claim distinction as a racer, a power, a speed, that a simple race cannot make him exercise ; perhaps the superior science of a player who cannot skate as well as another, may enable him to surpass that man in general speed, by minimizing his work and by allowing him to husband his strength

DEFENCE OF THE GOAL—Stopping the puck with the hand.

for the great efforts that occur at different stages of the game.

When a forward skates down the rink near the side, his easiest way of dodging an opponent is by caroming the puck against the boards, which act as a cushion, passing his man on the outside, and recovering the puck which bounces out to meet him. In this play the puck should invariably be lifted, because the dodge is expected, and if the puck slides along the ice to the side it may often be easily stopped.

When a forward, rushing down the ice, is well followed by another of his side, he should not try to dodge the cover-point, but should draw out that man by inclining to the side, and pass the puck to his partner, taking care to then place himself in the best possible position to receive it back, if the latter cannot shoot.

A man should check his opponents' stick heavily, as a gentle stroke, an easy check, has seldom any effect.

Experiences teaches that in a low, bent position, a man can get up speed a good deal quicker than when he keeps his body upright, and. moreover, he is less liable when skating thus, to suffer from the body check of an opponent.

A body check means the striking of a man with your hip or shoulder in order to cause him to stop or even fall. The most effective check of this kind is striking a man with the hip, upon his hip, because this is more or less the centre of gravity in a human being, and a good, solid weight catching a person in this spot, especially when that person is balancing on his skates or rushing up the ice, seldom fails in the desired result. The forward player who indulges in body-checking makes a fatal mistake, for although he may gain a momentary advantage, he wastes so much energy in the act, that in the long run he is a heavy loser. This is an incontrovertible fact, the testimony any forward will bear out the statement. He should avoid body-checking with even greater care than he should being checked, because the former requires a great effort, and the latter only seldom injures the man who is encountered. A defence man, however, who has but few rushes up the ice, can afford to enjoy the pleasure of "throwing" himself at an opponent, and often to great advantage. He is in a good position to catch his adversary "on the hip," especially when the latter is "on the wing," as it were, and can thus often put a short stop to a dangerous run. The effect of a body-check is not so "striking" when the object of·it steadies himself in as low **a** position as possible, while the man who is using the play attains his end better by catching his opponent, as stated above, in the centre of his weight, or higher, when the latter is not steadily placed. This practice of body checking is permissible, and, to a certain degree, scientific, but it is questionable whether it be not a less noble way of overcoming a dangerous opponent, than by expert stick handling, or by some gentler means. It cannot be said to be directly in accordance with the strictest, the highest sense of polished, fair, scientific play. It certainly is a feat, difficult of accomplishment, to stop a man who is rushing towards you with the speed of an express train, and upset him without the slightest injury to yourself, but is this the fairest way of defending your flags? It savors too much of roughness, and can be the cause of a serious accident, because a fall on the ice, at any time is usually painful and dangerous enough, without any additional impetus from without. If it is allowable, it is most unfair to "body" a man into the side of the rink.

Among some of the senior teams the practice of interference is becoming prominent, and should be severely checked, because it is an·unfailing cause of unnecessary roughness. No player, however mild, who is rushing down the ice to secure an advantageous position, will allow himself to be deliberately interrupted, stopped by an opponent who has not, and should not have the right to oppose his course, without picking a bone or two with him. Another innovation that is calculated to injure the game, is mass plays. This rupture of the rules was conspicuous among certain teams last year. It might be hard to imagine or detect such a thing in hockey, but it, nevertheless, occurs. It is practically, "concentrated interference," in technical terms, and, as in foot ball, is used by the team which attempts to score, a point which distinguishes it from simple interference as used by an attacked team to prevent scoring. To be properly carried out it involves the disregard for the rule regulating on-side movements, and is therefore, though difficult to detect, a breach of the same. The teams in cities where the practice of interference in foot ball is more popular, are the most given to this play.

It is essential that the two centre men and the right wing should be able to shoot the puck as well from the right side as from the left.

because the chances of scoring in either ways are about equal. As for the left wing, he is called upon so seldom to shoot from the right, that is presuming that he holds his stick correctly, with the blade to his left side, that it is not so important for him.

The most dangerous, successful lift for the goal, is raising the puck about to the level of the knee. This height is too great to allow the goaler's stick to be of any use, and is not high enough to be stopped by his bulky body.

The lift is not obtained by strength, but by knack and a good stick. Of course the more strength there is in the act of lifting the greater will be the velocity of the shot. But strength minus knack is not so successful as knack minus strength.

To lift the puck, the edge of the blade of the hockey stick must touch the puck lower than half its thickness, and the practiced "twist of the wrist" accomplishes the rest. This form of ridding yourself of the rubber is most important, because by a lift the puck travels farther and faster than it would along the ice, which gets cut up soon after the opening of a match, besides, it is much harder for an opponent to stop a lift than an ordinary sliding puck.

It is a mistake to lose courage because your opponents score the first three or four goals.

Do not begin to play roughly because you are losing ; and do not purposely and ostentatiously avoid scoring against a team that has already lost, because even if a bad beating does discourage them they would rather suffer it than be humiliated by any such show of pity.

Do not imagine that after winning a few games the match is won, because "accidents" occur, and do not dream of laurel wreathes and championships on account of your success in the opening of the series.

Attend every practice but do not become overtrained.

A man should not lose his temper because he suffers a sore knock. A display of "fireworks" is often the cause of an undesirable rest among the spectators.

Do not question the decision of the umpire or referee. Let your captain plead the case.

THE PLAY-OFF

PROTECTING THE GOAL

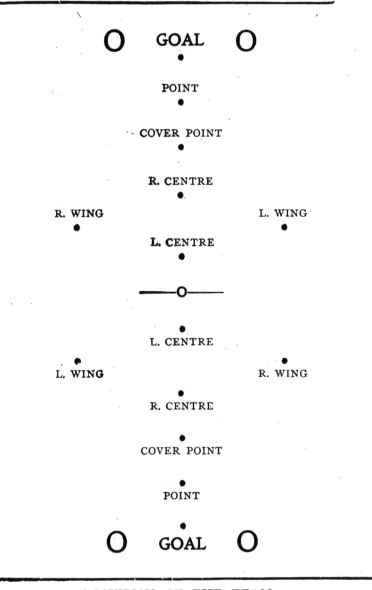

POSITIONS OF THE TEAM.

THE TEAM

The hockey team is composed of seven players, each of whom has his own, distinct position to fill, and the success that attends a well balanced aggregation, depends a great deal upon the systematic way in which these positions are looked after.

Each man has his particular place to fill, his own work to do, and each position on the team, from the goal-minder's to that of the centre forward, differing essentially from the others in the duties that it entails, calls for work that may not be used in any other.

I.—THE GOAL-MINDER.

Of all the responsible positions on a team, that of the goal-minder is perhaps the most difficult satisfactorily to fill. It is so hard to stop a strong, well-directed shot, and so many of them pour in during the course of a match, that in the exercise of his work, even though it occurs only periodically, the goaler is called upon to use the greatest skill and coolness. A forward may miss a good chance to score, and the effect is only negative ; a point or cover-point man may make a mistake, but there is usually an assistant around to help him ; but when the goal minder makes a blunder, the whistle is blown and a point is placed to the credit of his opponents.

Mr. F. S. Stocking, goal-keeper of the Quebec team, and generally recognized throughout Canada as the peer of his position, has kindly contributed the following hints on goal-minding :

" Goal-keeping is one of the easiest and at the same time one of the most difficult positions to fill successfully on the team.

" It is simple because it is not altogether essential to be an expert skater or stick handler It is difficult because it requires a quick and true eye together with agility of motion and good judgment.

" Besides keeping his eye on the puck, he must have a good idea where his opponents are placed so as to be prepared to stop a shot resulting from a sudden pass in front of goals.

THE PROPER METHOD OF STRIKING THE PUCK.

"I am of the opinion that the goaler should only leave his goal under the following conditions :—First, when he is quite sure that he can reach the puck before an opponent, and when none of his own team are near enough to secure it instead ; secondly; when one of the attacking side has succeeded in passing the defence and is coming in (unsupported) towards the goal, then the goaler, judging the time well, may skate out to meet him, being careful that he is directly in line between the shooter and goal. This sudden movement surprises the man and he is liable to shoot the puck inaccurately or against the goaler's body.

"In stopping the puck, the feet, limbs, body and hands are all used according to the nature of the shot. The stick is used to clear the puck from the goals after stop has been made, but rarely to make the stop.

"Some goalers use the hands much more frequently than others and make splendid stops in this way. But this depends on the individual's handiness, those accustomed to play base ball and cricket excelling.

"The most difficult shot to stop results from a quick pass in front of goals at the height of about one foot off the ice.

"Goalers should use a good broad bladed skate, not too sharp, so as to allow easy change of position from one side to the other of the goal. He should dress warmly and protect his body and limbs with the usual pads which at the same time help to fill up the goal.

"He must not get 'rattled' by the spectators and never lose confidence in himself."

Many a goal is scored by an easy, lazy, slide, or by a long lift, when the goaler is not expecting danger, therefore the man in this position should be careful to follow the movements of the puck even when it is at the other end of the rink, and cautious in stopping the easiest shot, because "there's many a slip." Nothing should fluster a goal keeper, nothing discourage him. If one of his opposing forwards dodges every one of his opponents, and has a clear, dangerous opening for the goals, even then let the goaler retain his self-possession and confidence, because, nine times out of ten, the forward who is making the attack is more excited over the peculiar circumstances of his rush than the former possibly could be, and will often shoot

THE IMPROPER WAY OF STRIKING THE PUCK.

less accurately than he would under less favorable conditions. It is a mistake for a goal-minder to imagine that he is not doing his duty because three or four or more points have been scored against him, because the fault may, and very often does, rest upon the poor sssistance he receives from his defence and forwards.

He should insist upon his defence men keeping at a reasonable distance from the goals, but if they do crowd in upon him, he should crouch down as low as the law allows and carefully watch the puck.

When the play is to his left, he should incline to that side in his goals, touching the pole with his leg and his side, and, if to the right, vice versa, but when it is directly in front, let him be right in the centre of his goal, occupying as much space as possible. He should never rely upon his assistants to stop any shot, but should always be prepared for an emergency. As soon as he stops the puck he should clear to the side, not waiting to be attacked, or if he has plenty of time, lift it towards his opponents' goals, although it is advisable to give it to one of his defence men to deal with, because, through practice, they can usually lift better than he, and, besides, are in a position to start a rush by passing it to their forwards.

A poor skater who is a good goal-minder would be a better goal-minder if he were a good skater. His skates should be made in such a manner, or fastened with straps in such a way, that the puck may not pass between the plate and the blade, and his stick should be short in the handle so that he may manage it easily when the puck is near his skates.

II.—THE POINT.

Mr. " Mike " Grant, the best known player in Canada, captain for years of the erstwhile invincible Victorias, in speaking on general defence work, says :—

" The defence of a successful team must necessarily be as proportionately strong as the forward line. Although their territory, their sphere of action, is more limited than that of their forwards, the defence men have work to do that is, in its effect, as important as the rushes of the latter.

" The goal-keeper should consider that he is enclosed in a magic circle, and should scarcely ever leave his position, but if he does he should return to it as soon as possible. He should not depend upon

POSITION OF STICK FOR SHOOTING PUCK.

his defence to stop the puck. The point and cover-point should play as if they were one man in two positions. The position of the point should be determined by that of the cover-point. If the cover-point is on one side, the point should be on the other to such an extent only, though, that each may have an equally good view of the play, and that a forward who advances toward their goals will have two distinct men to pass, instead of two men, one directly and close, behind the other.

"When two forwards approach their goals, the cover-point should devote his attention to the man who has the puck and block him as well as he may, and the point should advance slightly to meet the other, and, incidentally, to intercept any pass that may be attempted.

"During a tussle behind or to the side of the goals, the point and cover-point should never leave their positions vacant. If the one leaves his place the other should remain in front, but never should both be away, because the absence of these two men from their proper positions is the cause of more games being lost, than any other fault they may commit.

"The position of the point man is essentially defensive. The distance between him and the goaler is determined by the proximity of the play. He should not stray too far from his place, because oftentimes he is practically a second goal-minder, able, through the practice that his position gives him, to stop almost equally well as the latter, but although he should remain close to his goal-keeper, he should never obstruct that man's view of the puck. Whenever it becomes necessary for the goaler to leave his place, it is the duty of the point man immediately to fill it, and remain there until the latter returns.

"He should, as a rule, avoid rushing up the ice, but if he has a good opening for such a play he should give the puck to one of his forwards on the first opportunity and then hasten back to his position, which has been occupied in the interim by the cover-point.

"When it is absolutely necessary, combination play may be carried on by the point and cover-point in front of goals, but only with the greatest care.

"When three or four forwards skate down together it is advisable for the defence men to retire towards their goals and block them until assistance from the forwards arrives.

POSITION OF STICK FOR LIFTING PUCK.

" The defence men should not allow themselves to be coaxed, drawn out, by their opponents.

" A lifting competition between the defence men of the opposing teams is fatiguing to the forwards, and very tiresome to look at.

" The position of the cover-point is the best adapted for the captaining of a team, because a man in this place is in touch with the defence and the forward players."

III.—THE COVER-POINT.

Mr. Hugh Baird, captain and cover-point of the Montreal Hockey team, contributes the following in connection with the position, in which he has risen to such high distinction :

" The cover-point is a combination of a defence man and a forward, and is allowed, in virtue of the fact, more latitude with respect to leaving his position than any man on the team, except the rover.

" In his capacity of a defence player he should linger arouud his goals as long as the puck is near, and be very careful when he secures it in front of the poles. When the play is at the other end of the rink, the cover-point should advance to about the middle, so that when the puck is lifted down he may return it without loss of time, in order to keep the game centered around his opponents' goals and to save his forwards the trouble of skating up to him so that they may again 'get into play.' It is by playing far up under these circumstances that a clever cover-point can shine to the advantage of his team. If he has a good opening, he should shoot well for the goals, but if he has not he should, as I have said, return the puck instantaneously.

" When in this position, far from his goals, a cover-point is suddenly confronted by an opposing forward who rushes down the ice, he should skate towards his defence, watching that man and gradually closing in upon him.

" I am an advocate of legitimate body-checking, and consider that the most successful way of stopping a man who approaches alone is by blocking him—obstructing his course in any way that does not violate Section 8. It requires less effort and is less dangerous to block an opponent than to ' body ' him.

" A forward player, nine times out of ten, or even oftener, will try

SHOOTING AT GOAL WITH GOAL-KEEPER AND POINT DEFENDING.

to pass the cover-point by first feinting to the left, then dodging to the right. If this be remembered, the cover-point will not bother about that feint to the left, which is to his right, but will almost invariably expect to be passed on his left, or the forward's right, and will act accordingly.

"He should be as careful to prevent a forward player who is advancing towards him from sliding the puck between his feet, a common and successful dodge; which, however, in its execution requires a good deal of confidence on the part of the man who attempts it.

"The puck should be stopped, from a lift, by the hand, and in such a way that it will drop 'dead' and not bound forward.

"In lifting the puck, attention should be given to direct it so that it shall not be sent to an opponent, but to the side or to an opening, in order to enable the forwards to follow it up and block the return.

"It is advisable for the defence to be so placed that if the cover-point is directly in front of the goal-minder the point will be either to the left or right, between the two, because they will thus all have a clear view of the play. On no occasion should the three defence men be in Indian file—one directly in front of the other.

"A cover-point, in lifting the puck, should be guided by the positions of his players. If they are around his opponents' defence, he should quickly lift the puck in their direction, in order to keep the play in that territory. In this case he should lift, and not dribble or slide the puck, because a lift is more difficult for his adversaries to secure. If his forwards are around his own defence and he is forced clear, he should shoot the puck in such a direction that will cause his opponents the most trouble to recover it, thus enabling his forwards to follow up with a chance of securing the return.

"When the cover-point secures the puck, and only a short distance exists between himself and his forwards, he should advance, pass the puck to them and bring them all into play, then return to his post.

"He should attempt an individual rush only when an exceptional opportunity offers itself. In the early part of a match the cover-point should not leave his position more than is absolutely necessary, but towards the end, when his opposing forwards are played out he may assume, to great advantage, a decidedly offensive position.

"The stick of a cover-point should be somewhat heavier than a ferward's. It should be long in the handle, in order to increase a man's reach, and the blade should taper, becoming thinner towards the end, which aids in raising the puck. His dress and skates are the same as used by the forwards."

IV.—THE FORWARD.

Mr. Harry Trihey, of the Shamrock Hockey Team, and perhaps the most effective forward player in the game, gives the following as his opinion regarding forward playing:

" The essentials of a forward are science, speed, coolness, endurance and stick-handling, which embraces shooting, and the success of a forward line is combination play. Science and speed are exercised at all times during the game; coolness is essential, especially when a forward is near his opponents' goals; endurance is taxed in the second half of the match, and stick-handling is a necessary quality whenever the player has the puck.

" The centre player, the right and the left wing men must stick closely to their positions, but the rover, as his name indicates, may use his judgment as to what particular place is most in need of extra help. If the defence be weak or crippled, the rover should lend his aid to that part of the team when he is not absolutely needed by the forwards, but he should also follow up every rush that is made by the latter. He should be the busiest man on the team, because, as a forward, he must attack, and follow up every attack on his opponents' goals; he should also be the particular player to return to help his own defence against every rush by his adversaries.

" It is necessary that a forward should be in the 'pink of condition,' and that he should take great care of himself in practice, because even the slightest injury will proportionately lessen his usefulness. Besides the ordinary training, it is advisable to diet, in order to get into the proper condition. 'Early to bed, early to rise,' should be a player's maxim, because sleep before midnight is much more beneficial than it is after that time.

" Dodging depends upon the ingenuity of a player, and no rule can be laid down to regulate the science, because each separate dodge must be adapted to the circumstances of his own and his opponents' positions.

" To resist a body-check a player should take care to make himself as solid on the ice as he can, but at the same time allowing the upper part of his body to remain limber, so that the shock may not be so strongly felt. When advancing towards a man who, he knows, is going to body-check him, a player should, on meeting him, slide the puck forward to such a place, and in such a manner, that after the encounter, he may have a better chance of recovering it. I think, however, that a clever forward can nearly always avoid a body-check, because, advancing at a high rate of speed, he has the advantage over an opponent who awaits him. The forward should never body-check, because this exhausts his strength.

" The most successful shot for the goals is a lift which raises the puck only as high as the goal-minder's knee. A player should accustom himself to shoot from both sides.

" Most goals are scored on a rush, not from a scrimmage, and for this reason it is advisable not to lose too much energy in tussling for the puck behind the goal-line.

" It is a mistake to attempt to score a game when too far removed from the goals, or at too great an angle to the side.

" The forwards should be careful not to ' bunch,' not to crowd around the puck, which can be avoided if each man plays in his own position.

" A forward's dress and skates should be light.

" His stick should be strong, light and not too flexible, having a long blade and handle, which will increase his reach. It should be made of second growth ash, which is the most serviceable wood, because it combines strength with lightness, and does not, like most other woods, absorb the water which frequently appears on the ice. When a player gets a stick that suits him, he should carefully note its particular points, so that when that one breaks, he may secure others of the same shape. A player should use the stick that he himself prefers, and should not be guided by the choice of others, although, of course, he should always look for an improvement of his own."

THE REFEREE.

In describing the qualifications and duties of a referee, Mr Gordon Lewis, of the Montreal Victorias, whose efficient services in this position make him a competent judge on the subject, has this to say :

" The man who accepts this important position should, above all, have a thorough knowledge of the rules of the game, because, in his capacity of referee, he must judge the play and carefully guard against any infringement of the rules. His decision is final, his authority supreme, and although he should listen attentively to any objection that a captain of a team may have to his ruling, he must judge conscientiously according to his own interpretation of the rules. A referee should never argue with a player, because the captain is the only man on the team who is entitled to raise an objection. It is my opinion that a referee cannot very well be too strict. It is his duty, it is to the interest of the game, to exact that the game be played according to the rules.

" He should follow the play from one end of the rink to the other, keeping in the centre, when the puck is near the side, and *vice versa*, but always near enough to follow it well, without ever obstructing the way.

" He should be strictly impartial, and should be guided, in his decisions only by stern justice ; besides, he should be careful that the crowd does not in any way influence him. Even a losing team should be allowed no advantage, however slight.

" Before the match begins, the referee ought to warn the players against rough and foul play—and afterwards deal out his punishment to an offender commensurately with the grievousness of the foul.

" Loafing off-side should be strictly dealt with, as also should deliberate rough play. A referee in enforcing the rules should give his decision only after careful consideration, but then he should remain firm, obdurate, unless, perhaps, he plainly sees that he has made a mistake, which even a referee may do, in which case it might be well for him to reverse his ruling.

" If the two centre men will not face correctly, let them be changed, and if the next couple are bothersome, they should be ruled off.

" If the referee sees evidence of unfairness on the part of the umpires it is his duty to warn the captains.

"As a general rule, the referee should be very strict on the 'off-side' question, but I think that in the case. where the off-side is a matter of only a few inches, and the play is not in the vicinity of the goals, a little leniency in this respect will make the game more interesting."

AMERICAN AMATEUR HOCKEY LEAGUE

RAPID ADVANCES OF GAME HAS MADE IT A NATIONAL PASTIME.

The great game of hockey has made such rapid strides in the United States in the last few years that it has now become looked on as one of our national pastimes. Like all other games, hockey has made its most beneficial advances while under regularly organized direction. The game is primarily one for amateurs, although in some parts of the country professionalism of a more or less marked degree has taken root from time to time. The game as conducted by the American Amateur Hockey League is pleasingly free from evidences of professionalism, and this organization it is that is responsible for the healthful growth of hockey, particularly in the eastern part of the United States.

The American Amateur Hockey League was formed in 1896, and many of the men who aided in its inception had won repute as patrons of the sport during several years preceding that date.

The clubs originally forming the Hockey League were the New York Athletic Club, Crescent Athletic Club of Brooklyn, the St. Nicholas Skating Club of New York, and the Brooklyn Skating Club. Bartow S. Weeks was elected the first president and Carroll Post was made vice-president.

During the season of 1896-97 the New York Athletic Club seven displayed the best form and won the championship.

During the season of 1897-98 the Hockey Club was admitted, as also was the Montclair Hockey Club. In 1897-98 the New York A. C. team again won the championship.

Throughout the next season, 1898-99, the Crescent Athletic Club remained in the league, but its team did not participate in the matches. The Brooklyn Skating Club captured the championship with the creditable total of eight wins and no defeats.

During the next season, that of 1899-1900, the Crescent Athletic Club re-entered the game with redoubled energy, and won the championship of the league. Montclair had no team entered in the game, but nevertheless retained its membership, as the Crescents had done during the season before. In place of the Montclair seven, the team of the New York Naval Reserves was admitted.

The Naval Reserves retired in the following season, that of 1900-01. The Quaker City team of Philadelphia was admitted to the league. The home games of that club were played in the Ice Palace rink. The Quakers remained in the league one year, finishing last. During this season the Crescents again captured the championship by winning eight games and losing two. The seven of the New York A. C. finished second.

In the next two seasons, that of 1901-02 and that of 1902-03, the Crescents were also victorious. No new teams were admitted during these two seasons, nor were any dropped.

Dissatisfaction arose among hockey players of the New York Athletic Club and in the season of 1903-04 certain players of the Mercury Foot organization transferred their allegiance to the St. Nicholas Skating Club. It happened that some of the directors of the St. Nicholas Skating Club were also prominent officials in the New York Athletic Club and consequently they objected to the presence of the New York Athletic Club men on the St. Nicholas team. Consequently they, these men from the New York Athletic Club and various members of the St. Nicholas Club, cut loose from the last-named organization and formed a new hockey club. To this hockey club was given the name Wanderers.

Through the action of the men who became the Wanderers the St. Nicholas Skating Club lost men on whom it placed much dependence and consequently the club went without a team during this season. Throughout the season, however, the St. Nicholas Club retained its membership in the league. The Wanderers played strongly during the season and won the championship.

The St. Nicholas Hockey Club was reorganized last season to take the place of the Wanderers and won the championship.

Before the American Amateur Hockey League was formed the game was played by many able skate manipulators on McClane's Pond, about a mile above Van Cortlandt Park. Many games were played there in the early 90's. The Montclair team came over from New Jersey to play, and a team from Baltimore frequently journeyed there. The New York Hockey Club, the St. Nicholas Skating Club, and the Metropolitans were prominent New York organizations. Later the New York Athletic Club adopted the entire New York Hockey Club team and started a hockey seven for the purpose of playing the St. Nicholas team. The Metropolitans and the New York Hockey Club afterwards amalgamated and became the Hockey Club of New York.

CONSTITUTION

OF THE

AMERICAN AMATEUR HOCKEY LEAGUE

ARTICLE I.

The name of this organization shall be "The American Amateur Hockey League."

ARTICLE II.

Its object shall be to improve, foster and perpetuate the game of Hockey in the United States; protect it from professionalism; and to promote the cultivation of kindly feeling among the members of Hockey Clubs.

ARTICLE III.

SECTION 1. Its officers shall be a President, a Vice-President, a Secretary-Treasurer, and an Executive Committee not exceeding four, to be elected annually by ballot, who shall be entitled to vote the same as delegates by virtue of their office. They shall hold office until their successors are appointed. No Club shall be allowed to have more than one representative as an officer or member of the Executive Committee of this League.

SEC. 2. Any vacancy occurring in the Executive Committee may be filled at a regular meeting of the said Committee.

SEC. 3. All officers shall be ex-officio members of the Executive Committee.

SEC. 4. Two members of the Executive Committee shall be appointed by the Executive to be a Special Committee, which shall be known as the Governing Committee.

ARTICLE IV.

Section 1. The President shall preside at all meetings of the Association and Executive. He shall have a vote in the election of officers and the admission of new Clubs, and the casting vote in a tie. He shall call special meetings of this League whenever he deems them necessary, or when requested in writing to do so by any two Clubs in the Association, who shall specify their reasons for desiring such meeting.

Sec. 2. The Vice-President shall perform the duties of the President in his absence.

Sec. 3. The Secretary-Treasurer shall keep an accurate record of the proceedings of the League and the Executive Committee, a register of the clubs in the League, and the names of office bearers, and the address of the Club Secretary. He shall conduct all correspondence of the League and the Executive, keep a record of the decisions of the latter on all points of appeal, protest and complaint. He shall notify all officers and clubs of their election, issue all notices of meetings, keep a correct account of moneys received and disbursed by him, and report to the League. He shall bank all funds in trust.

Sec. 4. The Executive Committee shall view and decide upon all business submitted to them and shall generally manage the Association; provided, however, that nothing herein contained shall give the Executive Committee jurisdiction over matters coming within the scope of the Governing Committee, unless same come before the Executive Committee in appeal.

Sec. 5. The Governing Committee shall hear all appeals, protests and complaints, and decide all questions, arising during the championship season, relative to the eligibility of players, disputes between contesting clubs or teams, appeals against rulings of match officers or otherwise, and generally take full charge, control and management of the championship games and all club members of this League.

ARTICLE V.

Section 1. The convention shall be composed of two delegates from the several Amateur Hockey Clubs in the United States, which have been duly admitted to membership, each delegate shall have one vote.

SEC. 2. Delegates must be in good standing in the Club they represent.

SEC. 3. No delegates shall be admitted to the convention unless he shall have filed with the Secretary a certificate of his appointment signed by the President and Secretary of the Club he represents.

ARTICLE VI.

SECTION I. Clubs in this League must be composed exclusively of Amateurs.

DEFINITION OF AN AMATEUR.

SEC. 2. An Amateur is one who has never competed for a money prize or staked bet, or with or against a professional for any prize, or who has never taught, pursued, or assisted in the practice of athletic exercise as a means of obtaining a livelihood; or who has never entered any competition under a name other than his own.

SEC. 3. The Amateur rule of the A. A. U. is adopted by this League and embodied in this Constitution.

SEC. 4. No club shall be admitted to membership in this League unless it adopts in its Constitution the words or sentiments in this article.

ARTICLE VII.

SECTION I. Any Hockey club desiring to join this League shall send to the Secretary an application for membership, not later than November 1st, also as many copies of its Constitution and By-Laws as there are clubs in the League, a list of its officers, and number of members, together with membership fee as prescribed in Article VIII.

ARTICLE VIII.

SECTION I. The annual fee for each club member of this

League shall be $10.00, payable when applications for membership in the League is made and at each annual meeting thereafter.

SEC. 2. Any club whose fee shall remain unpaid later than January 1st in any year shall not be entitled to representation or to vote at any meeting; nor be represented by any team in the Championship series; and shall be considered to have forfeited all right to membership in this League.

ARTICLE IX.

SECTION 1. Any club wishing to make an appeal, protest or complaint to the Governing Committee, must within three days from the time at which the cause of complaint, appeal or protest occurred, submit to the Governing Committee in writing (in duplicate), a full and detailed account of the matter in appeal, protest or complaint signed by the President and Secretary of the complainant club. All such appeals, protests or complaints shall be accompanied by the sworn statements of all witnesses in support thereof. Such complaint shall be mailed postage prepaid by registered letter to the Chairman of the Governing Committee, who shall within one day of receipt of same, mail one copy thereof in like manner to the Secretary of the club complained against. Within three days of the receipt of any such appeal, protest or complaint, the answer of the responding club must be in the hands of the chairman of the Governing Committee duly signed by the President and Secretary of such club, accompanied also by the sworn statement of all witnesses to be used in reply to such appeal, protest or complaint. A failure to make appeal, protest or complaint, or to answer as hereinbefore provided, shall finally and absolutely debar the defaulting club of a hearing.

SEC. 2. The Governing Committee shall at once meet and consider the appeal, protest or complaint and within three days after receipt of reply render its decision in the premises and forthwith notify both clubs by registered letter as above provided. Such decision shall in all cases be final, and without appeal, except as hereinafter provided.

SEC. 3. Any club wishing to appeal from the decision of the Governing Committee may within three days after receipt of decision as provided in Section 2 of this article, take appeal to the Executive Committee, in the following manner:

The club so desiring to appeal shall at the same time furnish the Secretary of the Association with two copies of its appeal, protest or complaint (with sworn statements of its witnesses) signed by the President and Secretary of such club, and shall deposit with him the sum of $25.00.

Upon these conditions being complied with, the Secretary of the Association shall immediately forward one copy to the club complained against, which shall within three days make reply to such appeal, protest or complaint, and submit sworn statements of its witnesses. The Secretary of the Association shall then call a meeting of the Executive to be held within three days, stating the object of such meeting.

Both clubs shall submit their briefs of evidence at this meeting and the decision of the Executive on a two-thirds vote of those present on the hearing of the appeal, protest or complaint shall be final. If the decision be in favor of the complaining club, the deposit of $25 shall forthwith be returned, but if the decision be adverse, the deposit shall be forfeited to the League.

SEC. 4. The Executive on motion may direct both clubs to appear with their witnesses for examination orally by the Executive, or any such appeal.

ARTICLE X.

SECTION 1. The League may suspend or expel any player or any Club for notorious or continued foul play or unfair conduct, or for any persistent infringement of the laws of the game or the rules of the League.

SEC. 2. Any player or any Club so suspended may be readmitted by making an ample official apology, in writing, to the Executive Committee and promising future compliance with the Constitution and By-Laws of the League.

ARTICLE XI.

SECTION 1. The League shall hold its annual Convention on the second Thursday in November, in the City of New York.

Sec. 2. Clubs shall be notified of time and place of meeting at least two weeks previously.

ARTICLE XII.

Section 1. No amendment or alteration shall be made in any part of the Constitution, except at the annual Convention of the League and by a three-fourths vote of the members present. Notice of and full particulars of any proposed alterations or amendment must be made to the Secretary of the League, in writing, and by him communicated to the Clubs in its membership, in writing, at least two weeks before it can be voted upon. When notice of alteration or amendment has been given, as above, both the notice and amendment thereto may be voted upon at the Annual Convention.

Sec. 2. Eight delegates shall form a quorum at the Annual Convention.

Sec. 3. The League shall have the privilege of limiting the number of Clubs in the League.

AMERICAN AMATEUR HOCKEY LEAGUE
LAWS OF HOCKEY.

SECTION 1. The game of Hockey shall be played on ice by two teams, the players of which shall all be on skates. Its object shall be the lawful scoring of goals. The team scoring the greater number of goals during the playing period shall be declared the winner.

RINK.

SEC. 2. A hockey rink shall be at least 112 by 58 feet. The imaginary lines at the two ends of the rink shall be termed the goal lines. The two sides of the rink shall be known as the side lines.

GOALS.

SEC. 3. A goal shall be placed midway on each goal line, and shall consist of a goal net supported by two upright posts 4 feet in height, placed 6 feet apart, and at least 10 and not more than 15 feet from the edge of the ice. The goal posts must be firmly fixed to the ice.

NOTE.—In the event of a goal post or net being broken or displaced, the referee shall at once stop the game and not allow play to be resumed until after the damage is repaired.

POSITIONS.

SEC. 4. There shall not be more than seven players on a hockey team. These players shall fill the position of goal, point, cover point and forwards, respectively. The goal position shall be the one that is directly in front of the goal. At no period during the play shall any player who fills this position, lie, kneel, or sit upon the ice. He must also always maintain a standing position. The point position is the one that is directly in front of the goal position. The cover point position is the one directly in front of the point position. The four forward positions shall be known as the left wing, the right wing, the center and the ·over, respectively. The wing positions shall be at the two ends of the forward line. The center position is the one mid-way on the forward line, and it shall be the duty of the player who fills this position to face the puck. The rover position is between the cover point and the center positions.

NOTE.—It is to be understood that the positions herein named are the ones that the players are supposed to fill when the teams face off in the center of the ice.

STICKS.

SEC. 5. A hockey stick shall not be more than three inches wide at any part and not more than thirteen inches long at the blade. It shall be made entirely of wood. Tape binding is permissible, however. Each player shall carry a hockey stick in his hand, and shall be considered out of the play the moment he violates this rule.

SKATES.

SEC. 6. No player shall wear skates that are pointed or sharpened in such a manner as to be unnecessarily dangerous to other players. The referee shall be the judge, and shall refuse to allow a player to use such skates.

PUCK.

SEC. 7. A puck shall be made of vulcanized rubber one inch thick throughout. It shall be three inches in diameter, and shall weigh at least 7 6/16 and not more than 7 9/16 ounces.

OFFICIALS.

SEC. 8. There shall be a referee, an assistant referee, two goal umpires and two timekeepers for each match. Should a referee be unable to continue to officiate, his assistant shall become the referee. The referee shall fill all vacancies in other official positions that may occur during a match; or when the competing teams have been unable to agree; or when the selected officials are absent at the advertised starting hour. In the event of a dispute over the decision of an umpire, the referee may remove and replace the official.

DUTIES OF THE REFEREE.

SEC. 9. The referee, before starting a match, shall see that the other officials are in their proper places. He shall see that the ice is in condition for play and that the goals comply with the rules. He shall order the puck faced at the commencement of the game and at such other times as may be necessary. He shall have full control over the puck during the match. He shall call offside plays. He shall have the power to rule off for any period of the actual playing time that he may see fit any player who violates the rules. The referee shall, furthermore, perform all other duties that may be compulsory.

DUTIES OF THE ASSISTANT REFEREE.

SEC. 10. The assistant referee shall see that no player violates Section 19 of the Laws. He shall have the power to rule off for any period of the actual playing time that he may see fit any player who violates said section. The assistant referee shall become the referee should the latter be unable to continue to officiate.

DUTIES OF THE UMPIRES.

SEC. 11. An umpire shall be stationed behind each goal. He shall inform the referee whenever the puck has passed between the goal posts from the front. He shall have no jurisdiction over the awarding of a goal. He shall stand upon the ice, and shall retain the same goal throughout the entire game.

DUTIES OF THE TIMEKEEPERS.

SEC. 12. The timekeepers shall keep an accurate account of the time of the match, deducting time for stoppages in actual play. They shall immediately report to the referee any variance in time, and the referee shall decide the matter. The timekeepers shall keep an accurate account of penalties imposed, and no penalized player shall return to the ice without the permission of the timekeepers. The timekeepers shall be notified by the referee when a goal is scored, and shall keep an accurate record of the tallies. The final score shall be given by them to the referee at the close of the match. They shall, at half time, notify the contesting teams when five and when eight minutes have expired. They shall at half time, notify the referee when ten minutes have expired.

LENGTH OF GAME.

SEC. 13. There shall be two halves of twenty minutes each, with an intermission of ten minutes between the two periods of play. At the end of the forty minutes' play, should the score be tied the teams shall change goals, and play shall be resumed at once and continued until a goal has been scored. Should the tie remain unbroken at the expiration of twenty minutes of extra play, the referee shall declare the game a draw. The referee must start each period on schedule time.

SEC. 14. Time shall be taken out whenever the game is suspended by the referees, and shall begin again when the puck is put in play. No delay of more than five minutes shall be allowed.

SUBSTITUTES.

SEC. 15. Substitutes shall be allowed only in the case of an injury. In the event of any dispute as to the injured player's ability to continue, the matter shall at once be decided by the referee. Should any player be compelled to leave the game during the first half, his side shall be allowed a substitute. Should an injury occur during the balance of the game, the opposing team may either drop a man or allow a substitute in the place of the injured player. A player who has been replaced by a substitute shall not return to further participation in the game.

In exhibition or practice matches this rule may be altered by the captains.

WHAT CONSTITUTES A GOAL.

SEC. 16. A goal shall be scored when the puck shall have lawfully passed between the goal posts. No goal shall be allowed that is the direct and immediate result of loafing offside, an offside play, a kick or a throw by the hand. The referee shall

decide upon these points, and may render his decision even after
the puck has passed between the goal posts.

FACE.

SEC. 17. A face shall consist of the referee placing the puck
upon the ice on its largest surface between the sticks of two
players, one from each team. The referee shall then order the
play to begin. Should a player repeatedly refuse to lawfully
face the puck, he shall be penalized by the referee. A face shall
take place in the center of the ice at the beginning of each period
and after the scoring of each goal. The referee may also order
a face at any time and place he deems necessary. A face shall
be in order whenever play is resumed.

OFFSIDE PLAY.

SEC. 18. Any player nearer to his opponent's goal line than
is an imaginary line running through the center of the puck
and parallel with the two goal lines is offside. A player offside
shall be considered out of the play, and may not touch the puck
himself or in any manner prevent any other player from doing
so, until the puck has been touched by an opponent in any way
whatsoever, or until it has been carried nearer than he is himself to his opponent's goal line. If a player violates this rule,
the puck shall be faced where it was last played before the off-
side play occurred. In the event of the puck rebounding off the
body of the player in the goal-keeper's position, the other players
of his team shall be considered on side.

FOUL PLAYING.

SEC. 19. There shall be no unnecessary roughness. No player
shall check another from behind. No player shall throw his
stick. No player shall trip, hold with his hand or stick, kick,
push or cross-check an opponent. No player shall interfere in
any way with an opponent who is not playing the puck. No
player shall raise his stick above his shoulder, except in lifting
the puck. No player shall use profane or abusive language or
conduct himself in an unsportsmanlike manner. A player being
out of the play shall not interfere with an opponent.

PUCK FOULS.

Sec. 20. A player may stop the puck with any part of his stick or body. He may not, however, hold, bat, throw, kick or carry the puck with his skate or any part of his body. He may not close his hand upon the puck. The player in the goal position may catch the puck, but if he does he must at once drop the puck to the ice at his own feet.

WHEN THE PUCK LEAVES THE ICE.

Sec. 21. When the puck goes off the ice or a foul occurs behind the goal line, it shall be brought out by the referee to a point five yards in front of the goal line, on a line at right angles thereto, from the point at which it left the ice or where the foul occurred, and there faced. In the aforementioned cases the puck shall always be faced at least five yards to the left or the right of the nearer goal post. When the puck goes off the ice at the side lines it shall be taken by the referee to a point five yards out at right angles with the nearer side line and there faced.

PENALTIES.

Sec. 22. In awarding a penalty the referee or his assistant shall use discretion in order that his ruling does not work against the better interests of the non-offending team.

CHAMPIONSHIP RULES.

Section 1. All games shall be played under the rules adopted by the American Amateur Hockey League.

Sec. 2. The playing season shall be from December 1 to March 31, both days inclusive.

Sec. 3. The championship shall be decided by a series of games, a schedule of which shall be drawn by one delegate from each Club to the annual convention. The Club winning the greatest number of matches shall be declared the champion.

Sec. 4. All championship matches shall be played on rinks arranged for by the Executive Committee of the American Amateur Hockey League.

SEC. 5. The League shall offer a championship trophy, the winning Club to hold same and to be recognized as the Amateur Champion of the United States. The trophy shall be delivered to the winning Club within seven days after the close of the season. Any Club winning the championship for three years, not necessarily in succession, shall become the permanent owner of the trophy.

SEC. 6. Any team making default shall forfeit its right to compete for the championship and be liable to a fine of $100 unless good reasons can be shown to the Executive Committee for defaulting. In case of default by any team all matches which have been scheduled for this team shall be credited as victories to its opponents. This rule shall also be applied in case of expulsion.

SEC. 7. In all matches the Governing Committee shall appoint the referee and his assistant unless it has received written notice from either of the two Clubs at least three days before the match that they have agreed on the two officials.

SEC. 8. It shall be the duty of the captains of the contesting teams to hand to the referee previous to the start of each match the names of his players written on forms supplied by the Secretary of the League. The referee shall fill in the date of the match and the names of contesting Clubs, substitutes used, if any, the score at the end of the match, with names of other officials, the whole to be duly signed by himself and forwarded immediately to the Secretary of the League.

SEC. 9. A player must have been an actual resident within fifty miles of the place in which his Club is located for at least sixty days previous to being eligible to appear in any League match, and must be a bona fide member of the Club he represents at least thirty days before he is eligible to compete in any championship match. No player shall play in any Amateur Hockey League schedule match, who, during the then current season, has played with another Club in a recognized Hockey Association without special permission of the Executive.

SEC. 10. The Secretary of each Club shall file with the Secretary of the American Amateur Hockey League at least thirty days prior to opening of the championship season a list of the players of his Club. The Secretary of each Club shall also file with the Secretary of the American Amateur Hockey League the names of any additional players immediately upon their being elected to membership.

SEC. 11. All matches must be stared at 8.30 p. m., and if for any reason there be any delay in the commencement of a match the Club at fault shall pay to the League as a penalty the sum of $10, unless good reason be given for such delay. The referee is to see that this rule is observed and to notify the League within two days should any breach of it occur.

SEC. 12. The puck used in all championship matches must be the official puck of the League.

SEC. 13. Goal nets must be approved by the Executive Committee of the League.

ONTARIO H. A. RULES

1. The game is played on ice by teams of seven on each side, with a puck made of vulcanized rubber, one inch thick all through and three inches in diameter.

STICKS.

2. Hockey sticks shall not be more than three inches wide at any part, and not more than thirteen inches long at the blade. They shall consist entirely of wood, with tape binding permissible.

GOAL.

3. A goal is placed in the middle of each goal line, composed of official goal nets supported by two upright posts, four feet in height, placed six feet apart, and at least five feet from the end of the ice. The goal posts shall be firmly fixed. In the event of a goal post or net being displaced or broken, the referee shall blow his whistle, and the game shall not proceed until the post or net is replaced. It shall be the duty of the referee before each match to measure the goals.

MATCH.

4. Each side shall have a captain (a member of his team), who, before the match, shall toss for choice of goals.

5. Each side shall play an equal time from each end, a ten minutes' rest being allowed at half time. The duration of championship matches shall be one hour, exclusive of stoppages. The team scoring the greater number of goals in that time shall be declared the winner of the match, subject to the qualifications contained in Rules of Competition, No. 15. If at the end of that time the game is a draw, ends shall be changed and the match continued for ten minutes, each side playing five minutes from each end with a rest of five minutes between such five minute ends, and if neither side has then scored a majority of goals, similar periods of ten minutes shall be played, in the same way until one side shall have scored a majority of goals.

TIME-KEEPERS.

6. Two time-keepers shall be appointed, one by each captain, before the commencement of the match, whose duty it shall be to keep an accurate account of the time of each game, deducting time for stoppages in the actual play. They shall immediately report to the referee any variance in their time, and the matter shall be at once decided by him. The referee also shall appoint a time-keeper, who shall keep the time of penalized players, and shall direct them to enter the game. The time-keepers shall be under the control of the referee. A gong shall be kept for their use.

REFEREE.

7. There shall be only one referee for a match, and in no case shall he belong to either of the competing clubs, and he may be an amateur or a professional. He is to enforce the rules; adjudicate upon disputes or cases unprovided for by rule; appoint or remove goal umpires; control the time-keepers; keep the score, announcing each goal as scored; and at the conclusion of the match declare the result. The puck shall be considered in play until the referee stops the game, which he may do at any time, and which he must do at once when any irregularity of play occurs, by sounding a whistle. His decision shall be final.

SCORE.

8. A goal shall be scored when the puck shall have passed between the goal posts from in front and below the tops of the posts.

GOAL UMPIRES.

9. There shall be one umpire at each goal; they shall inform the referee when the puck has been put into the goal from the front.

FACE.

10. The game shall be started and renewed by the referee blowing his whistle or calling "Play" after dropping the puck in the centre of the ice between the sticks of two players, one from

each team, who are to face it. After a goal has been scored the puck shall be faced in like manner in the centre of the ice.

OFF-SIDE.

11. A player shall always be on his side of the puck. A player is off-side when he is in front of the puck, or when the puck has been hit, touched or is being run with, by any of his own side behind him (i. e., between himself and the end of the rink near which his goal is placed).

A player being off-side is put on-side when the puck has been hit by, or has touched the dress or person of any player of the opposite side, or when one of his own side has run in front of him, either with the puck or having played it when behind him.

If a player when off-side plays the puck, or annoys or obstructs an opponent, the puck shall be faced where it was last played before the off-side play occurred. A player on the defending side shall not be off-side when he takes a pass from or plays the puck as it bounds off his goal-keeper within a space of three feet out from goal and extending to the side of the rink.

KNOCKING-ON.

12. The puck may be stopped with the hand but not carried or held or knocked on by any part of the body.

CHARGING, TRIPPING, ETC.

13. No player shall raise his stick above his shoulder. Charging from behind, tripping, collaring, kicking, cross-checking, or pushing shall not be allowed. And the referee must rule off the ice, for any time in his discretion, a player who, in the opinion of the referee, has deliberately offended against the above rule. If a player makes any unfair or rough play, or disputes any decision of the referee or uses any foul or abusive language, the referee may rule him off for the remainder of the game or for such time as he may deem expedient, and no substitute shall be allowed.

WHEN THE PUCK LEAVES THE ICE.

14. When the puck goes off the ice behind the goal line it shall be brought out by the referee to a point five yards in front of the goal line. on a line at right angles thereto, from the point at which it left the ice, and there faced.

When the puck goes off the ice at the side, it shall be similarly faced three yards from the side.

GOAL-KEEPER.

15. The goal-keeper must not during play, lie, sit or kneel upon the ice; he may stop the puck with his hands, but shall not throw or hold it. He may wear pads, but must not wear a garment such as would give him undue assistance in keeping goal. The referee must rule off the ice, for any time in his discretion, a player, who, in the opinion of the referee, has offended against this rule.

CHANGE OF PLAYERS.

16. No change of players shall be made after a match has commenced. Should any player be injured during a match, break his skate, or from any other accident be compelled to leave the ice, the opposite side shall immediately drop a man to equalize the teams and the match proceed, without such players until such time as the player so compelled to leave the ice is ready to return. In event of any dispute, the matter shall at once be decided by the referee.

STOPPAGES.

17. Should any match be stopped by the referee by reason of any infringement of any of the rules or because of an accident or change of players, the puck shall be faced again at the spot where it was last played before such infringement, accident or change of players shall have occurred.

LAWS ACROSS BORDER

CONDITIONS WHICH GOVERN PLAY OF THE EASTERN CANADA LEAGUE.

SECTION 1. A team shall be composed of seven players who shall be bona fide members of the clubs they represent. No player shall be allowed to play on more than one team in the same series during a season, except in a case of bona fide change of residence from one city to another at least fifty miles apart.

SEC. 2. The game shall be commenced and renewed by a face in the center of the rink.

DEFINITION CF A FACE.

The puck shall be faced by being placed between the sticks of two opponents, and the referee then calling "play."

The goals shall be placed at least ten feet from the edge of the ice.

SEC. 3. Two half-hours, with an intermission of ten minutes between, will be the time allowed for matches, but no stops of more than fifteen minutes will be allowed. A match will be decided by the team winning the greatest number of games during that time. In case of a tie after playing the specified two half-hours, play will continue until one side secures a game, unless otherwise agreed upon between the captains before the match. Goals shall be changed after each half-hour.

SEC. 4. No change of players shall be made after a match has commenced, except for reasons of accidents or injury during the game.

SEC. 5. In the event of a player being injured or compelled to leave the ice during a match, he may retire from the game for the period of ten minutes playing time, but play must be continued immediately without the teams leaving the ice, the opposing team dropping a player to equalize. If at the expiration of ten minutes the injured player is unable to resume his position on the ice, his captain may put on a substitute, providing the injury occurred during the first half of the match. If, however, the player was injured during the second half, the opposing captain shall have the option of dropping a man for the balance of the playing time or allowing the injured player's side to put on a substitute. The man dropped to equalize shall return to the ice when the injured player does or when substitute is put on. In the event of a dispute between the captains as to the injured player's fitness to continue the game, the matter shall at once be decided by the referee, and his decision shall be final. An injured player may not resume play after his place has been filled by a substitute, without the consent of the opposing team's captain.

Sec. 6. Should the game be temporarily stopped by the infringement of any of the rules, the captain of the opposite team may claim that the puck be taken back and a face take place where it was last played from before such infringement occurred.

Sec. 7. When a player hits the puck, anyone of the same side, who at such moment of hitting is nearer the opponent's goal line is out of play, and may not touch the puck himself or in any way whatever prevent any other player from doing so, until the puck has been played. A player should always be on his own side of the puck. In the event of the puck rebounding off the goal keeper's body, players of his team touching the puck are to be considered on side.

Sec. 8. The puck may be stopped but not carried or knocked on by any part of the body, nor shall any player close his hand on, or carry the puck to the ice in his hand. No player shall raise his stick above the shoulder, except in lifting the puck. Charging from behind, tripping, collaring, kicking or shinning shall not be allowed, and for any infringement of these rules, the referee or his assistant may rule the offending player off the ice for that match, or for such portion of actual playing time as he may see fit, but it shall not be necessary to stop the game to enforce this rule.

Sec. 9. When the puck goes off the ice or a foul occurs behind the goals it shall be taken by the referee to five yards at right angles from the goal line and there faced. When the puck goes off the ice at the sides it shall be taken by the referee to five yards at right angles from the boundary line and there faced.

SEC. 10. The goal keeper must not during play, lie, kneel or sit upon the ice, but must maintain a standing position.

SEC. 11. Goal shall be scored when the puck shall have passed between the goal posts from in front below an imaginary line across the top of posts.

SEC. 12. Hockey sticks shall not be more than three inches wide at any part.

SEC. 13. The puck must be made of vulcanized rubber, one inch thick all through and three inches in diameter.

The Spalding hockey puck, the official puck of the League, must be used in all matches. The home club to furnish the referee with a new puck previous to the match.

SEC. 14. The captains of the competing teams shall agree upon two timekeepers, one penalty timekeeper, two umpires (one to be stationed behind each goal, which position shall not be changed during a match). In the event of the captains failing to agree on umpires and timekeepers, the referee shall appoint them.

SEC. 15. All disputes during the match shall be decided by the referee, and he shall have full control of all players and officials from the commencement to finish of matches, inclusive of stops, and his decision shall be final.

SEC. 16. All questions as to games shall be settled by the umpires, and their decision shall be final.

SEC. 17. In the event of any dispute as to the decision of an umpire or timekeeper the referee shall have power to remove and replace him.

SEC. 18. Any player guilty of using profane or abusive language to any officials or other players shall be liable to be ruled off by the referee or his assistant for the match or for such portion of actual playing time as he may see fit.

SEC. 19. The referee shall, previous to the commencement of the match for which he has been duly appointed or agreed upon, obtain from the captains of each of the competing clubs a full list of the players of their respective teams, and, if during the match a substitute is used by either club, the captain of the club using such substitute shall give to the referee the name of such substitute player, and same will be inclined in the list of names of said team.

The referee shall, before starting a match, see that the necessary penalty timekeeper, timekeepers and umpires have been appointed and are in their respective places. In the event of the competing clubs failing to agree upon umpires and timekeepers the referee shall appoint same. The referee shall have full control of all officials and players during the match (including stops), he shall face the puck at the commencement of each half and at such other times as may be necessary, he shall also call off-sides or rule offending players off for such period of playing time as he may see fit, and perform such other duties as may be provided for hereinafter or in the laws of hockey or championship rules.

The referee shall order the teams on the ice at the advertised time, and if for any reason there be more than fifteen minutes delay in the commencement of the match, the referee shall state in his report to the Secretary of the Association the cause of the delay, and name the club or clubs if they be at fault. It will be the referee's duty to record the time of the starting and finishing of the match, as well as the games scored, mailing to the Secretary of the Association, within three days of date of match, on the forms provided for the purpose, a report of the match in detail, including the names of players penalized, together with the number and length of penalties imposed (this information to be obtained from the penalty timekeeper, who shall also keep for the referee a record of the games scored, and, if possible, who by and the time).

Should the assistant appointed or agreed upon be made to act at the last minute, or through sickness or accident be unable to finish the match, the referee shall have power to appoint another in his stead, if he deems it necessary or if requested to do so by the captains of one of the competing teams.

Sec. 20. The assistant referee will during the period of a

match be under the control of the referee; he shall, however, have full power to stop the game should an offside or foul occur which has escaped the notice of the referee. He shall also have power to rule off for such time as he may see fit any player committing a foul. He shall also perform such other duties as may be assigned to him by the referee from time to time. If owing to illness or accident, the referee is unable to continue to officiate, the assistant shall perform such duties as devolve upon the referee during the balance of the match, selecting an assistant if he deems it necessary or if requested to do so by the captain of one of the competing teams.

SEC. 21. The penalty timekeeper shall keep a complete record of the penalties imposed by the referee or his assistant, and shall have control of all players while serving the time of their penalties, and any player ruled off shall not return to the ice until the playing time for which he was penalized has expired and then only by permission of the penalty timekeeper.

A record of the games scored, who scored by and the time of each shall be recorded by the penalty timekeeper, and this, together with a record of the penalties imposed, shall be handed the referee at the close of the match.

EASTERN CANADA RULES

SECTION I. The season shall be from the first of January to the tenth of March, both days inclusive.

SEC. 2. The championship shall be decided by a series of games, a schedule of which shall be drawn up by one delegate from each club at the annual convention. The club winning the most matches shall be declared champions.

SEC. 3. Unless President is notified jointly by the competing clubs at least four clear days before a match, that a referee and assistant have been agreed upon and have consented to act, the appointments shall be made at a meeting of a committee composed of one delegate from each club, to be called three days previous to the date set for each game. In the event of a tie, the President or his representative to have casting vote.

SEC. 4. All championship matches shall be played in rinks arranged for by the home club, subject to the approval of the Association. Rink must be at least one hundred and seventy-five feet long by sixty-five feet in width. Goals shall be six feet wide and four feet high, and provided with goal nets, such as approved by the Association. The goals shall be placed at least ten feet from the edge of the ice.

SEC. 5. The home club shall furnish the referee with a new puck for each match. The Spalding Hockey Puck, the official puck of the league, must be used in all matches.

SEC. 6. All matches shall be started at 8.30 P. M., unless otherwise agreed upon by the competing clubs, and if, for any reason, there be more than fifteen minutes' delay in the commencement of a match, the club at fault shall, unless good reasons be given to the President for the delay, pay to the Association as a penalty the sum of twenty-five dollars. The referee shall state in his report to the Secretary of the Association if more than fifteen minutes' delay occurred in the commencement of the match, giving cause of such delay and naming the club at fault. Upon receipt of this information the President shall decide whether or not the club be fined.

SEC. 7. Visiting clubs shall be allowed traveling expenses (by the home club) as follows: Between Montreal and Ottawa, eighty-five dollars; between Montreal and Quebec, one hundred dollars; between Ottawa and Quebec, one hundred and twenty-five dollars.

SEC. 8.—The Association shall offer a championship trophy, the winning club to hold same, and be recognized as champions. The trophy shall be delivered to the winning club within seven days after the close of the season.

SEC. 9.—Any club winning the championship three times shall become absolute owners of the trophy.

SEC. 10. Any team making default shall forfeit the right to compete for the championship for that season, no matches played with defaulting clubs shall count. Unless a written notice signed by the President and Secretary of the club be sent to the Secretaries of the opposing team and Association, five days previous to the match, signifying the club's intention to default, the defaulting club shall pay to the opposing team within thirty days a fine of one hundred dollars.

HISTORY OF THE STANLEY CUP

The Stanley Cup is the most important of the many hockey trophies in Canada. It was donated by Lord Stanley of Present to the hockey world, the chief condition being that it was to be played for by champions of leagues, its possession to denote the championship of Canada. It was in 1895 that the cup was first played for. The Amateur Hockey Association of Canada was first given custody of the trophy. This was in the middle of the season played against Queens, of Kingston, then the Ontario champions, the Montreal team winning. At that period of the Ontario Hockey Association's history, the Kingston College was a member of the body, leaving some years afterwards on the formation of the Intercollegiate league. After Montreal had won from Queens, Victorias won the championship of the league and gained possession of the trophy.

The first surprise in the cup series was that furnished by the Winnipeg Victorias who dropped into Montreal and on February 14, 1896, defeated Montreal Victorias by a score of 2 to 0, and the white metal bowl went west for the first time. That Peg team was a revelation in the East, and it was a great team too. Whitty Merritt played in goal, Flett and Higginbotham in front, while the forward line was composed of Jack Armitage, Howard, Dan Bain, and Campbell. The team they defeated was something of a class lot too. Moon Jones played in poles, Henderson and Mike Grant in front. The forward line was formed of Bob Macdougall, Wallace, McLea, and Davidson, and in the second half Hartland Macdougall replaced Wallace.

The Davidson who played on the team was Shirley Davidson, a graduate of McGill University, and noted in Canadian hockey and rugby. He was also a sailor and achieved international fame by participating in some of the early struggles on Lake St. Louis for the defence of the Seawhanka Cup. In August of the current year, 1907, Mr. Davidson lost his life in a drowning fatality in which a young lady of a foremost Montreal family was also drowned. By a sadly curious coincidence another famous player who figured in Stanley cup matches, lost his life in the water. This was Hod Stuart. He was a native of Ottawa and played on the Ottawa team. Being in the contracting business, he moved to Quebec and played there. Afterwards he went to Pittsburg and acted as manager of the professional team. Early in the season of 1906-07 Stuart was induced to leave Pittsburg and go to Montreal to play for Wanderer. For this he received a compensation of $1,200 for which he played the regular series matches, ten in number, and three Stanley Cup contests. In the summer he went to Brockville to engage in work there. He was a strong swimmer and was accustomed to have a dip every day. One day he swam out to the lighthouse and dived from the pier. He dived into four feet of water, struck a rock and broke his neck. He was a capable player, speedy and cool, and well versed in the fine points. He was a general selection as cover point for the All-Canada team.

In December, 1896, the Montreal Victorias went after the prize and took it away from Winnipeg, scoring six goals to Peg's five. In those days a single match determined possession of the trophy.

A joke team challenged for the cup in 1897, the Capitals of Ottawa, being defeated in the Victoria Rink by 15 goals to 2.

In 1899 there was a challenge from Winnipeg Victorias, and at the request of the teams it was arranged that the series should be two games in three. The first match fell to the home team two to one, a sensational play by Graham Drinkwater being the feature of this match. In the second game there was a mix-up with the score three to two in favor of Montreal Victorias Tony Gingras, a wing player on the visiting team went to the ice, and it was claimed that he had been cut down by Bob Macdougall. The latter denied this, but the visitors refused to play unless Macdougall was punished. Mr. Jack Finley, who was referee, declined to do so, and after an argument he left the ice and went home. He was sent for and returned to the Arena, but the Victorias were obdurate in their refusal to play unless Macdougall was sent off. Finally the Westerners quit and the match and series was awarded to the Montreal Victorias.

At the end of the season of 1899 Shamrocks won the league championship, the final match being between Shamrock and Victoria, and was won by the Irishmen by the close score of

I to 0, Harry Trihey scoring the only recorded goal of the match. A challenge from Queen's University team, then champion of the Ontario Hockey Association, was accepted while the Shamrocks were on tour and they had to return from St. John to play the collegians. Queen's had a poor team, Jack Harty being the only player of any form on the line-up. The Presbyterians were beaten.

At the beginning of the following season the Halifax champions came to Montreal and met the Shamrocks. In two matches the Halogonians proved helpless against the Irishmen, then in their prime, and a total score of 21 goals was scored against 2 for the visitors.

In 1900 Winnipeg Victorias again challenged for the cup and played three matches in Montreal against Shamrocks. Winnipeg won the first match, 4—3; lost the second and third matches, 3—2 and 5—4.

The following year Winnipeg Victorias again came after the cup, and this time they took it from the Shamrocks, winning two matches. For these games Shamrocks played Mike Grant, who had then retired from the Victoria team, and was used because of the illness of Frank Tansey. The series was an exciting one, each match being scored by a goal.

Ottawa won the league championship, but did not go west after the cup.

After Winnipeg Victorias had defended the cup from Wellingtons, of Toronto, Montreal having won the championship in 1902, went after the mug, and landed it after a series of three games. Winnipeg Victorias came back after the cup, but were defeated in Montreal in a series which required four matches, one being a draw. In this match one of the visiting players was Freddie Scanlan, who previously had been with the Shamrocks in the defence and loss of the cup, and who then was living in Winnipeg. A Montreal player was Tom Phillips, who afterwards went west, and returned with Rat Portage, one of the finest teams ever sent east after the trophy.

When Ottawa won the championship in 1903, the cup went to them and stayed there until Wanderer won the league championship in 1906.

WHAT TO USE FOR ICE HOCKEY

There is nothing like having things exactly right. How much more satisfied you feel when you realize that no adverse criticism can be passed upon your outfit, and it gives you more confidence while you are playing, too. It is this feeling that the player has who uses Spalding goods, and those who appreciate them could not be induced to make a change no matter how great the pressure. Would you jeopardize the chance of winning a game for your team in order to save a paltry amount on a pair of skates or a stick? Or, if you did, could you ever forgive yourself if they lost because of this economy on your part? Of course, this is not written to justify you in purchasing an expensive outfit, where one at a more moderate price would answer the purpose, but merely to emphasize the fact that in selecting the outfit for any athletic sport, price is to a great extent a secondary consideration. The main point is: are the goods correct and will they give satisfaction?

The stick which is endorsed by the most famous players in the world is the Spalding Championship Hockey Stick No. o. It is made of finest selected Canadian rock elm, and for years past has been used exclusively by the champion teams of Canada. This stick costs 50 cents. This year we have added the Spalding "Autograph" Hockey Sticks to our line. These sticks are duplicates of those used by the most famous hockey players. The Forward and Defence models cost 75 cents each, while the Goal or "Built-up" models cost $1.00 each. The Spalding "Regulation" stick, No. 1, costs 40 cents, while the "Practice" stick, No. 2, made full size, costs 25 cents. The No. 3 is painted red, is made in boys' size and costs 25 cents. From this assortment the player can select with absolute certainty of satisfaction the stick most suitable to his purse.

When the subject of skates is discussed, the name which comes most readily to the lips of old and young is "Peck & Snyder," and there must be good reason for the long-continued popularity of

No. A1 Championship Pattern,

the skates manufactured under this brand. There has never been a time when they were not abreast of the times as to model, and the standard of quality has been maintained throughout even where prices have been reduced. Look no further when the Peck & Snyder Championship No. A1 Skate is shown you, because in this are embraced the good points of all the various models used by the most prominent players in former years—now the bulk of them use this style. The No. A1 Hockey Skate costs $5.00 per

No. 5H.

pair. In what is known as the Canadian pattern, and which is also to be fastened to the shoe with screws or rivets, there is the No. 5H, full nickeled and buffed, ribbed runners of three-ply welded steel, carefully hardened and tempered. These cost $3.50 per pair, while the No. 4H, similar in style, but with plain runners and with polished and blued tops, cost $2.50 per pair. After these in popularity come the skates with full clamp key fastenings, making it unnecessary for the player to keep a separate pair of shoes for hockey. The No. 7H is the best of this style, and is a very handsome skate, full nickel-plated and buffed, and with ribbed runners of three-ply welded steel. The No. 7H skates cost $4.00 per pair. A similar skate, but with plain runners and polished and blued tops, is the No. CH, which costs $3.00 per pair, while a good quality full nickeled skate, with full clamp fastenings also, is the No. DH, which costs $2.00 per pair. Surely this range of prices and styles should satisfy the most exacting.

An article which should not be lost sight of, not only in playing

Puck.

the game but also when purchasing the equipment, is the puck. The Spalding Trade Mark No. 13 puck has been adopted as the Official Puck by the Canadian Amateur Hockey League. It is made to conform exactly to the rules and costs 50 cents each. The Practice Puck No. 15, costs 25 cents each.

The Spalding Regulation Hockey Goals, made exactly right, costs $12.00 per pair. They are substantial, and there is no danger of an accident where they are set up, and they conform to the rules in every particular.

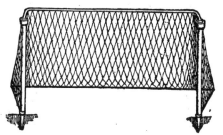

OFFICIAL RULES FOR ALL ATHLETIC SPORTS.

The following list contains the Group and the Number of the book of Spalding's Athletic Library in which the rules wanted are contained. See front pages of book for complete list of Spalding's Athletic Library.

Event.	Group	No.	Event.	Group	No.
All-Round Athletic Championship	12	182	Lawn Bowls	11	207
A. A. U. Athletic Rules	12	311	Lawn Games	11	188
A. A. U. Boxing Rules	12	311	Lawn Tennis	4	4
A. A. U. Gymnastic Rules	12	311	Obstacle Races	12	55
A. A. U. Water Polo Rules	12	311	Olympic Game Events—Marathon Race, Stone Throwing with Impetus, Spear Throwing, HellenicMethod of Throwing Discus, Discus,Greek Stylefor Youths	12	55
A. A. U. Wrestling Rules	12	311			
Archery	11	248			
Badminton	11	188			
Base Ball	1	1			
Indoor	9	9	Pigeon Flying	12	55
Basket Ball, Official	7	7	Pin Ball	12	55
Collegiate	7	312	Playground Ball	1	306
Women's	7	318	Polo (Equestrian)	10	199
Water	12	55	Polo, Rugby	12	55
Basket Goal	6	188	Polo, Water (A. A. U.)	12	311
Bat Ball	12	55	Potato Racing	12	311
Betting	12	55	Professional Racing, Sheffield Rules	12	55
Bowling	8	8			
Boxing—A. A. U., Marquis of Queensbury, London Prize Ring	14	162	Public Schools Athletic League Athletic Rules	12	313
Broadsword (mounted)	12	55	Girls' Branch; including Rules for School Games	12	314
Caledonian Games	12	55	Push Ball	11	170
Canoeing	13	23	Push Ball, Water	12	55
Children's Games	11	189	Quoits	11	167
Court Tennis	11	194	Racquets	11	194
Cricket	3	3	Revolver Shooting	12	55
Croquet	11	138	Ring Hockey	6	180
Curling	11	14	Roller Polo	10	10
Dog Racing	12	55	Roller Skating Rink	10	10
Fencing	14	165	Roque	11	271
Foot Ball	2	2	Rowing	13	128
Code of Rules	2	334	Sack Racing	12	55
Association (Soccer)	2	2 A	Shuffleboard	12	55
English Rugby	12	55	Skating	13	209
Canadian	2	332	Skittles	12	55
Golf	5	5	Snowshoeing	12	55
Golf-Croquet	6	188	Squash Racquets	11	194
Hand Ball	11	13	Swimming	13	177
Hand Polo	10	188	Tether Tennis	11	188
Hand Tennis	11	194	Three-Legged Race	12	55
Hitch and Kick	12	55	Volley Ball	6	188
Hockey	6	304	Wall Scaling	12	55
Ice	6	6	Walking	12	55
Field	6	154	Water Polo (American)	12	311
Garden	6	188	Water Polo (English)	12	55
Lawn	6	188	Wicket Polo	10	188
Parlor	6	188	Wrestling	14	236
Ring	12	55	Y. M. C. A. All-Round Test	12	302
Ontario Hockey Ass'n	6	256	Y. M. C. A. Athletic Rules	12	302
Indoor Base Ball	9	9	Y. M. C. A. Hand Ball Rules	12	302
Intercollegiate A. A. A. A.	12	307	Y.M.C.A. Pentathlon Rules	12	302
I.-C. Gymnastic Ass'n	15	333	Y.M.C.A. Volley Ball Rules	12	302
Lacrosse	11	201			
U. S. I.-C. Lacrosse League	11	305			

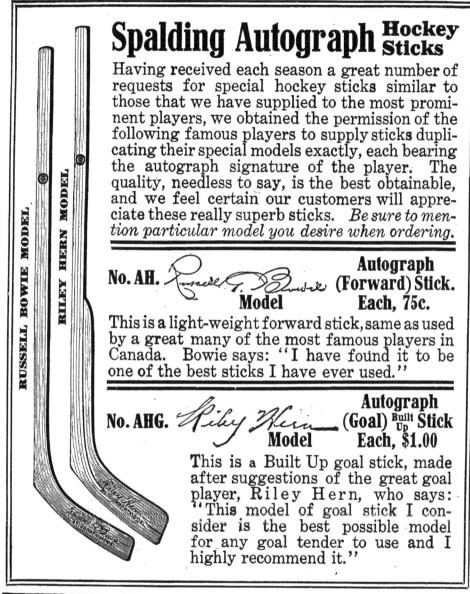

Spalding Autograph Hockey Sticks

Having received each season a great number of requests for special hockey sticks similar to those that we have supplied to the most prominent players, we obtained the permission of the following famous players to supply sticks duplicating their special models exactly, each bearing the autograph signature of the player. The quality, needless to say, is the best obtainable, and we feel certain our customers will appreciate these really superb sticks. *Be sure to mention particular model you desire when ordering.*

No. AH. *Russell T. Bowie* **Autograph (Forward) Stick.**
Model **Each, 75c.**

This is a light-weight forward stick, same as used by a great many of the most famous players in Canada. Bowie says: "I have found it to be one of the best sticks I have ever used."

No. AHG. *Riley Hern* **Autograph (Goal) Built Up Stick**
Model **Each, $1.00**

This is a Built Up goal stick, made after suggestions of the great goal player, Riley Hern, who says: "This model of goal stick I consider is the best possible model for any goal tender to use and I highly recommend it."

Spalding Autograph Hockey Sticks

Having received each season a great number of requests for special hockey sticks similar to those that we have supplied to the most prominent players, we obtained the permission of the following famous players to supply sticks duplicating their special models exactly, each bearing the autograph signature of the player. The quality, needless to say, is the best obtainable, and we feel certain our customers will appreciate these really superb sticks. *Be sure to mention particular model you desire when ordering.*

No. AH. *[signature: D. Phillips]* Model **Autograph (Forward) Stick. Each, 75c.**

This is a medium-weight forward stick, very fat on the bottom and with a very stiff handle. Strongly endorsed by the Captain of the famous Kenora team of Rat Portage, Ontario, former Champions of the world.

No. AH. *[signature: Lester Patrick]* Model **Autograph (Defence) Stick. Each, 75c.**

A long-handled defence stick, upright model. This player is very tall and plays the puck very close to himself.

TOM PHILLIPS MODEL

LESTER PATRICK MODEL

Spalding Championship
⊶⊷ Hockey Sticks ⊶⊷

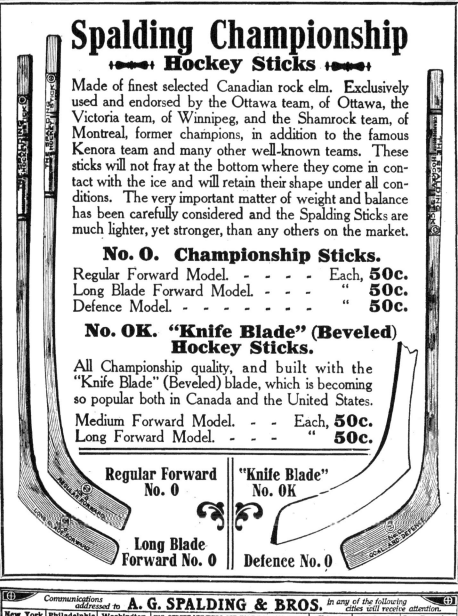

Made of finest selected Canadian rock elm. Exclusively used and endorsed by the Ottawa team, of Ottawa, the Victoria team, of Winnipeg, and the Shamrock team, of Montreal, former champions, in addition to the famous Kenora team and many other well-known teams. These sticks will not fray at the bottom where they come in contact with the ice and will retain their shape under all conditions. The very important matter of weight and balance has been carefully considered and the Spalding Sticks are much lighter, yet stronger, than any others on the market.

No. 0. Championship Sticks.

Regular Forward Model. - - - -	Each,	**50c.**
Long Blade Forward Model. - - -	"	**50c.**
Defence Model. - - - - - -	"	**50c.**

No. OK. "Knife Blade" (Beveled) Hockey Sticks.

All Championship quality, and built with the "Knife Blade" (Beveled) blade, which is becoming so popular both in Canada and the United States.

Medium Forward Model. - -	Each,	**50c.**
Long Forward Model. - - -	"	**50c.**

Regular Forward No. 0

"Knife Blade" No. OK

Long Blade Forward No. 0

Defence No. 0

Spalding Hockey Sticks

The Spalding Special "Built Up" Goal Stick

No. B. By adding to a selected Canadian rock elm goal stick a strip of elm, attached firmly, this "Built Up" style provides goal keepers with a stick that is up to the full limit of size allowed under the rules, yet it is scarcely any heavier than the ordinary forward style. Each, **$1.00**

Spalding "Regulation" Hockey Stick

No. 1. Made on the lines of our best grade Regular Forward Stick, and of selected and well seasoned timber. Very popular as an all-around stick. . . . . Each, **40c.**

Spalding "Practice" Hockey Stick

No. 2. Regulation size and made of good quality timber. A very serviceable stick. Each, **25c.**

Spalding "Youths'" Hockey Stick

No. 3. Smaller than Regulation and painted red. A very strong and serviceable stick for boys. Each, **25c.**

"Built Up"   "Regulation"

Special Pants for Forwards

No. 5B. Made of heavy Brown or White Canvas, hips padded lightly. Very loose fitting. Pair, **$1.00** ★ *$9.00 Doz.*

Spalding Hockey Pants—Unpadded
Fly Front, Lace Back

No. **1.** White or Black Sateen. Pair, **$1.25** ★ *$12.00 Doz.*

No. **2.** White or Black Sateen. Pair, **$1.00** ★ *$9.00 Doz.*

No. **3.** White or Black Silesia. Pair, **75c.** ★ *$7.50 Doz.*

No. **4.** White or Black Silesia. Pair, **50c.** ★ *$5.00 Doz.*

Stripes down sides any of these pants, **25c.** per pair extra. ★ *$2.40 Doz.*

Full Length Tights

No. **1A.** Full tights, best worsted, full fashioned, stock colors and sizes. Pair, **$4.00**

No. **605.** Full tights, cut worsted, stock colors and sizes. Pair, **$2.00** ★ *$21.00 Doz.*

No. **3A.** Full tights, cotton, full quality. White, Black, Flesh. Pr. **$1.00** ★ *$9.00 Doz.*

FULL TIGHTS

Spalding Eyeglass Protector for Hockey

Made of strong annealed wire, nicely padded, and a thorough protection for eyeglasses or spectacles. Each, **$2.00**

The prices printed in italics opposite items marked with ★ will be quoted only on orders for one-half dozen or more. Quantity prices NOT allowed on items NOT marked with ★

Spalding Patent Combined Shin and Knee Guard
(Patent Applied for)

No. 6

This guard is made with "barbette" piece of fiber, shaped to form of leg; special padding at knee cap, and sole leather formed knee protector. It extends down over ankle and is meant to be worn under stocking. Enthusiastically approved by the most prominent Hockey players in the United States and Canada. No. **6.** Pair, **$5.00**

Spalding Hockey Leg and Shin Guards

No. **4.** Leg Guards. Players' style, Leather. Pair, **$3.50**

No. **5.** Leg Guards. Players' style, Canvas. Pair, **$3.00**

No. **4G.** Leg Guards. Goal Tenders', Leather. Extra long and specially padded. Pair, **$4.50**

No. **5G.** Leg Guards. Goal Tenders', Canvas. Extra long and specially padded. Per pair, **$3.50**

Nos. 4G F and 40

No. **F.** Shin Guards equipped with ankle protectors. Canvas, 10 inches long. Pair, **$1.00** ★ *Dozen pairs, $10.00*

No. **40.** Shin Guards, equipped with ankle protectors. Leather, 10 inch. long. Pr., **$1.75** ★ *Doz. prs., $18.00*

Leg Guards for Goal and Defence

No. 1. Side View

No. **1.** A new design. With extra protection for calf and knee. Covered with best quality white mock buckskin. Per pair, **$4.50**

No. **9.** "Grand Prix" Skeleton style; with covering of superior quality tan cape leather. Per pair, **$4.00**

Spalding Regulation Ice Hockey Goals

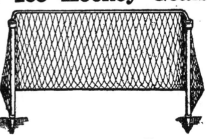

The importance of having goals that are substantially made and which conform exactly to the rules cannot be disregarded. Those that we furnish are duplicates of those used in the best rinks in Canada. Pair, **$12.00**

Spalding Official Hockey Pucks

No. 13. The Spalding Official Trade-Mark Puck has been adopted as the official puck of the Canadian Amateur Hockey League, composed of the following world-famed teams: Montreal, Shamrock, Quebec, Victoria and Westmount. . Each, **50c.**

See that our Trade-Mark appears on Puck itself before using.

Extract from Official Rules of the Canadian Amateur Hockey League: "SEC. 13. The Spalding Hockey Puck, the Official Puck of the League, must be used in all match games."

No. 15. The Spalding "Practice" Puck is regulation size, and really better than the so-called official pucks turned out by other manufacturers. . . . Each, **25c.**

Spalding Hockey Gloves

No. ES. "SIX FINGERED." Made of white buckskin, open palm, with extra long cuff and extra finger, giving full protection between thumb and first finger. Per pair, **$4.50**

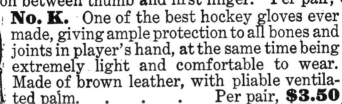

No. K. One of the best hockey gloves ever made, giving ample protection to all bones and joints in player's hand, at the same time being extremely light and comfortable to wear. Made of brown leather, with pliable ventilated palm. . . . Per pair, **$3.50**

No. K **No. L.** Unpadded drab buckskin gauntlet No. L glove. Extra long and a very popular style. Pair, **$2.50**

The Spalding Tubular Steel Hockey Skate

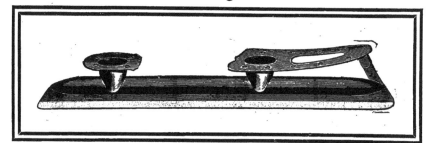

Made in exactly the same way as our Tubular Racing Skate. Strongly built but light in weight; all joints strongly reinforced. Blades made of chrome nickel steel, hardened and drawn, with edge 3-16 inch in width. Toe and heel plates are made with holes drilled so that skates may be fastened to shoes, and the plates are shaped. Sizes, 9½, 10, 10½, 11, 11½ inches, corresponding to same sizes in regular skates.

The Spalding
Tubular Steel Hockey Skate
Per pair, $3.00

The Spalding *Automobile*

An Improved Hockey Skate from Canada, the Land of Hockey

Hockey Skate

MADE WITH ALUMINUM TOP

PAT. MARCH 31, 1906.

This skate is made with special extra quality steel blade, but the top is of aluminum, making the weight much less than the ordinary all-steel hockey skate, but at the same time taking nothing away from the strength and durability. *Some of the best hockey players in Canada are using this style skate.*

No. BI. - For Men

SIZES: 9½, 10, 10½, 11, 11½, 12 inches.   Per pair, **$5.00**

No. BIL. For Ladies

SIZES: 8½, 9, 9½, 10, 10½ inches. . . Per pair, **$5.00**

Peck & Snyder's "Championship" Hockey Skate

The Skate that made the Game of Hockey famous

No. A1 CHAMPIONSHIP PATTERN

We were the first manufacturers to recognize the fact that for hockey players something more than an ordinary skate is required, and Peck & Snyder's Championship No. A1 Skate was gotten up after consultation with players on the champion hockey teams of Canada. It has been improved since its introduction by us, and today is recognized wherever hockey is played as the only skate that is suitable for hockey players with championship aspirations. Used by the leading hockey players in Canada and the United States. The blades are of the finest quality three-ply razor steel, hand forged and highly tempered. Extra heavy electro-nickel-plated and highly polished throughout. Each pair in box containing a piece of Selvyt polishing cloth for keeping the skates in perfect condition.

No. A1. Made in sizes 9½ to 11½ inches. Pair, **$5.00**

No. A1L. Ladies.' Like above, but small heel plate and narrow toe plate. Sizes, 9 to 11½ inches. Pair, **$5.00**

'Peck & Snyder's
Hockey Skates

Canadian Pattern

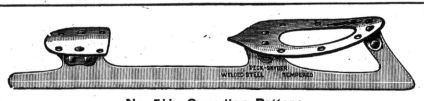

No. 5H. Canadian Pattern

Canadian Hockey Pattern. Finest quality three-ply welded steel runners. Carefully hardened and tempered.
Each pair in paper box.

No. 5H. Nickeled and buffed, ribbed runners. Sizes, 9½ to 11½ inches. . Per pair, **$3.50**

No. 5HL. Ladies'. Nickeled and buffed, ribbed runners. Small heel plate and narrow toe plate. Sizes, 8 to 10½ inches. . . Per pair, **$3.50**

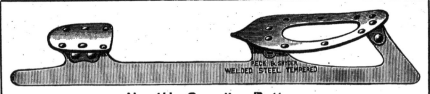

No. 4H. Canadian Pattern

Canadian Hockey Pattern. Plain runners of welded and tempered steel; nickel-plated and buffed.
Each pair in paper box.

No. 4H. Sizes, 9 to 11½ inches. Pair, **$2.50**

Peck & Snyder's Full Clamp Hockey Skates

THE full clamp fastening for hockey skates introduced by us some seasons ago has proven by its great popularity to be the style most adapted to the uses of players who do not find it convenient to keep a separate pair of shoes particularly for their hockey skates. The grades listed below are all made in this style.

No. **9H.** Full clamp fastening. Extra heavy nickel-plated and specially polished throughout. Blades of absolutely best quality three-ply welded steel, highly tempered, with ribbed flange at bottom. Made in both men's and women's models. Each pair in paper box, neatly wrapped. Sizes, 9½ to 12 inches. . . . . Per pair, **$5.00**

No. **9HL. Ladies'.** Like above, but small heel plate and narrow toe plate. Sizes, 9 to 11 inches. " **5.00**

No. **7H.** Nickel-plated throughout, not polished: ribbed runners. Sizes, 9 to 12 inches. " **4.00**

No. 9H

No. **CH.** Full clamp fastenings. Highly tempered and hardened three-ply welded steel runners. Each pair in paper box. Sizes, 9½ to 12 inches.
Per pair, **$3.00**

No. **DH.** Full clamp fastenings. Runners of best cast steel, hardened. Entire skate full nickel-plated. Each pair in paper box. Sizes, 9 to 12 inches.
Per pair, **$2.00**

No. CH

No. **CHL. Ladies'.** Same as No. CH, but small heel plate and narrow toe plate. Sizes, 8 to 11 inches. Pair, **$3.00**

No. DH

No. **EH.** Full clamp fastenings. Flat runners of best cold rolled steel. Entire skate nickel-plated. Each pair in paper box. Sizes, 9½ to 12 inches. Pair, **$1.50**

No. **EHL. Ladies'.** Same as No. EH, but with small heel plate and narrow toe plate. Sizes, 8 to 10½ inches. . . . . Per pair, **$1.50**

Peck & Snyder's "Special Ladies'" Hockey Skate

No. **CHLS.** Made with key clamp fastening in front and best quality leather heel strap. Flat runners of highly tempered and hardened three-ply welded steel. Each pair in paper box. Sizes, 8 to 10½ inches. . . . Per pair, **$3.00**

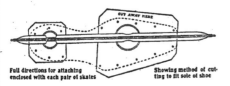

Peck & Snyder's
Ice Skates

YOU don't have to take anything for granted when you purchase a pair of Peck & Snyder's ice skates. Their reputation has been gained after a career of over forty years, and it is not a thing of simply a month or a year. Absolute honesty in manufacture has kept Peck & Snyder's Skates to the front since the first pair was made, and no change will be made in this policy while Peck & Snyder's Skates are continued on the market.

Peck & Snyder's "CHAMPIONSHIP" RACING AND SPEED SKATE

No. G. 16 and 18 inch blades, in sizes 10, 10½, 11 and 11½. All steel; tool steel ribbed blades, hand forged and highly tempered, ⅛-inch wide. Nickel-plated and polished throughout. Complete with straps. . . . Per pair, **$2.00**

Peck & Snyder's WOOD TOP SPEED SKATE

No. 5R. The speediest wood top racer. Beechwood top, rosewood finish, with nickel-plated heel, center and toe plates. Runners of welded steel, highly tempered and hardened, ¼-inch thick, nickel-plated. Sizes, 14, 16 and 18 inch runners. Complete with straps. . . . . Per pair, **$4.00**

No. 4R. Nicely varnished beechwood top, with nickel-plated heel, center and toe plates. Runners of best cast steel, hardened, ⅛-inch thick; bright finish. Sizes, 14, 16 and 18 inch runners. . . . . Per pair, **$3.00**

Peck & Snyder's WOOD TOP HOCKEY SKATE

No. 3R. Varnished beechwood top. Runners of cast steel, ¼-inch thick. Lengths of wood top, 10, 11 and 12 inches. Complete with straps. . . . Per pair, **$1.75**

Spalding's Athletic Library No. 304—"How to Play Ice Hockey." Written by a prominent Canadian expert. Price 10 cents.

Peck & Snyder's Rink Skates

BUILT STAUNCH AND TRUE·THEY NEVER FAIL

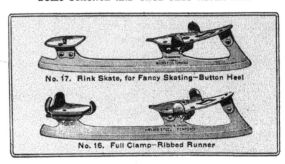

No. 17. Rink Skate, for Fancy Skating—Button Heel

No. 16. Full Clamp—Ribbed Runner

Photo by Gibson Art Galleries, Chicago.

AUGUST NELSON
Champion Western Fancy Skater
on Peck & Snyder's Rink Skates

Rink Skate, for Fancy Skating—Button Heel

The runners of these skates are absolutely the hardest made and have curved bottoms, as adopted by the leading skating clubs of this country

No. 17. Highly polished, nickel-plated and buffed, heel buttons; finest three-ply welded steel ribbed runners, extremely well tempered and concaved. Specially designed for fancy skating. Sizes 9½ to 12 inches. . . . . Per pair, **$5.00**

Full Clamp Rink Skates

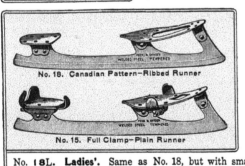

No. 18. Canadian Pattern—Ribbed Runner

No. 15. Full Clamp—Plain Runner

No. 16. Full clamp fastenings, highly tempered and concaved, three-ply welded steel ribbed runners. All parts heavily nickel-plated and highly polished. Specially designed for fancy skating. Sizes 9½ to 12 inches. Pair, **$5.00**

No. 16L. **Ladies'.** Same as No. 16, but with small heel plate and narrow toe plate. Sizes 8 to 10½ inches. . . Per pair, **$5.00**

No. 18. Foot plates same as on our Canadian pattern hockey skates; highly polished, nickel-plated and buffed throughout. Three-ply welded steel ribbed runners, well tempered and concaved. Sizes 9½ to 12 in. Pair, **$5.00**

No. 18L. **Ladies'.** Same as No. 18, but with small heel plate and narrow toe plate. Sizes 8 to 10½ inches. . . . . Per pair, **$5.00**

No. 15. Nickel-plated throughout, full clamp fastenings, runners of welded steel, hardened and tempered. Sizes 9½ to 12 inches. . . . . Per pair, **$3.00**

No. 15L. **Ladies'.** Same as No. 15, but with small heel plate and narrow toe plate. Sizes 8 to 10½ inches. . . . . Per pair, **$3.00**

No. 14. Nickel-plated, full clamp fastenings, runners of cast steel, hardened beveled edges. Sizes 9¼ to 12 inches. . . . . Per pair, **$1.50**

Communications addressed to	**A. G. SPALDING & BROS.**	in any of the following cities will receive attention.
New York Boston Syracuse Buffalo	Philadelphia Pittsburg Baltimore Montreal, Canada	Washington Atlanta New Orleans	FOR STREET NUMBERS SEE INSIDE FRONT COVER OF THIS BOOK	London, England Edinburgh, Scotland Sydney, Australia	Chicago Cincinnati Cleveland Columbus	St. Louis Kansas City Denver Detroit	San Francisco Seattle Minneapolis St. Paul

Prices in effect July 5, 1909. Subject to change without notice.

Peck & Snyder's Ladies' Ice Skates

The Special styles of Ladies' Skates which have been made by Peck & Snyder for over forty years past are even more popular to-day than they were a generation ago. They are graceful in form, have a special finish, and in all other respects are what they are intended to be—

PERFECT ICE SKATES FOR LADIES

No. **4-0L.** Welded steel runners, tempered, nickel-plated throughout; russet straps. Each pair in paper box. Sizes 8 to 11 inches.
Per pair, **$3.00**

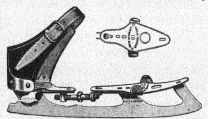

No. **00L.** Nickel-plated. Runners and other parts of best steel, nicely finished; russet straps. Sizes, 8 to 11 inches. Each pair in paper box. Per pair, **$1.60**
No. **0L.** Bright finish. Paper wrapped. **1.25**

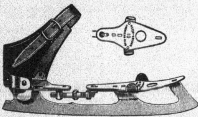

No. **1L.** Best cast steel runners, hardened. All parts nickel-plated; russet leather straps. In paper box. Sizes, 8 to 11 inches. Pr., **$2.25**

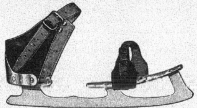

No. **19.** Made with steel runners and foot plates; russet leather straps. Each pair paper wrapped. Sizes, 8 to 11 inches. Pair, **90c.**

Spalding's Athletic Library No. 209—"How to Become a Skater." Fancy and Speed Skating. Illustrated with diagrams. 10 cents.

Peck & Snyder's Ice Skates

Remember, every Club Skate in use to-day is a direct copy from the original Peck & Snyder Skate invented over forty years ago. The boys who first wore Peck & Snyder's Skates grew out of them and passed them on to their sons, felt the same confidence in their quality as you do to-day, and with the same reason. You cannot take quality and reputation away from a reliable manufacturer. These stay by him long after patents expire.

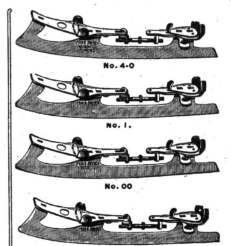

No. 4-0

No. I.

No. OO

No. O

No. **4-0.** Welded tool steel runners, hardened and tempered, nickel-plated throughout. Each pair in paper box. Sizes, 8 to 12 in. Pr., **$2.50**
No. **I.** Runners of best cast steel, hardened and nickel-plated throughout. Each pair in paper box. Sizes, 8 to 12 in. Pair, **$1.50**
No. **OO.** Runners of best cold rolled steel. Entire skate full nickel-plated. Each pair in paper box. Sizes, 8 to 12 in. . Pair, **$1.00**
No. **O.** Runners of best cold rolled steel. Entire skate bright finish. Each pair paper wrapped. Sizes, 8 to 12 in. . . Pair, **75c.**

Double Runner Sled Skates

No. **DR.** By using these skates it is possible to take a child on the ice without fear of injury. The runners are so wide apart that any child can stand on them easily. They are adjustable from 6 to 9½ in. and furnished with straps complete. Each pair in paper box. **50c.**

SCALE OF SIZES ON SKATES

The following will show the relative sizes of shoes and skates

SIZE OF SHOES	LENGTH OF SKATES
11, 11½	**8** inches
12, 12½, 13	**8½** inches
1, 1½, 2	**9** inches
2½, 3	**9½** inches
3½, 4, 4½	**10** inches
5, 5½, 6	**10½** inches
6½, 7, 7½, 8	**11** inches
8½, 9, 9½	**11½** inches
10, 10½, 11	**12** inches

Spalding's Athletic Library No. 304—"How to Play Ice Hockey."
Written by a prominent Canadian expert. Price 10 cents.

SPALDING SKATING SHOES

Spalding Ladies' Skating Shoes

These shoes are built as an athletic shoe should be, and the principles entering into their construction are the same as those which have made our men's skating shoes so popular. They will be found absolutely first-class in material, workmanship and design, are trim and neat in appearance and will give excellent satisfaction.

Spalding "Special" Skating Shoe

No. **336.** Best quality calfskin. Laces extra low at toe. Specially reinforced inside, obviating necessity for strap on shoe itself, but giving support where most required; full heel, leather lined tongue. **Per pair, $5.00**

Spalding Skating Shoe

No. **332.** Made of good quality calfskin, machine sewed. Has strap support over ankle outside, full heel. A substantial shoe in every detail. **Per pair, $3.50**

Spalding "Expert" Racing Shoe

No. **337** Fine quality material throughout and extremely light in weight; reinforced inside over ankles; leather very soft and easy; lacing extremely far down; very light sole. **Per pair, $5.00**

Spalding Racing Shoe

No. **338.** A racing shoe at a moderate price. Made after the design of our higher priced shoes, only differing in quality of material and construction. Light weight, and substantially made. **Pair, $3.50**

No. **350.** Ladies' Skating Shoe. Fine quality leather, nice and pliable. Reinforced with webbing inside to give support over ankle and at top; lacing extremely far down; full heel; neat toe; medium broad; good oak sole. **Pair, $5.00**

No. **330.** Ladies' Skating Shoe. Good quality, black leather. Full heel, laces down to toe, and has supporting strap-and-buckle over ankle. **Per pair, $3.50**

Spalding "Highest Quality" Sweaters

We allow four inches for stretch in all our sweaters, and sizes are marked accordingly. It is suggested, however, that for very heavy men a size about two inches larger than coat measurement be ordered to insure a comfortable fit.

WORSTED SWEATERS. Made of special quality wool, and exceedingly soft and pleasant to wear. They are full fashioned to body and arms and put together by hand, not simply stitched up on a machine as are the majority of garments sold as regular made goods. The various grades in our "Highest Quality" Sweaters are identical in quality and finish, the difference in price being due entirely to variations in weight. Our No. AA Sweaters are considerably heavier than the heaviest sweaters ever knitted and cannot be furnished by any other maker, as we have exclusive control of this special weight.

Colors: White, Navy Blue, Black, Gray, Maroon and Cardinal. Other colors to order. Prices on application. All made with 9-inch collars, sizes 28 to 44 inches.

No. **AA.** The proper style for use after heavy exercise, inducing copious perspiration for reducing weight or getting into condition for athletic contests. Particularly suitable for Foot Ball and Skating. Heaviest sweater made. . . Each, **$8.00** ★ *$84.00 Doz.*

No. **A.** "Intercollegiate," special weight. " **6.00** ★ *60.00 Doz.*

No. **B.** Heavy weight.
Each, **$5.00** ★ *$54.00 Doz.*

Spalding Shaker Sweater

We introduced this wool sweater to fill a demand for as heavy a weight as our "Highest Quality" grade, but at a lower price, and after much experimenting, we are in a position to offer it in the following colors only . Black, Navy Blue, Maroon, Gray or White. Sizes 30 to 44 inches.

No. **3.** Standard weight, slightly lighter than No. B. . . Each, **$3.50**

No. 3

Spalding Combined Knitted Muffler and Chest Protector

No. **M.** Made of special weight, highest quality worsted in solid colors. Gray, Black, Navy and Cardinal, to match our sweaters.
Each, **$1.00**

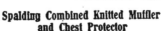
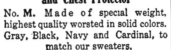

Front View   Back View

SPALDING WINTER SPORTS SWEATER

No. WJ

No. **WJ.** Most satisfactory and comfortable style for all winter sports; also useful for training purposes, reducing weight, tramping during cold weather, golfing, shooting, tobogganing, showshoeing; in fact, for every purpose where a garment is required to give protection from cold or inclement weather. Made with a high collar that may be turned down, changing it into the neatest form of a button front sweater. Gray only; in highest quality special heavy weight worsted. Size, 28 to 44 in. Each, **$7.50**

No. WJ with collar turned down

SPECIAL NOTICE—We will furnish any of the above solid color sweaters with one color body and another color (not striped) collar and cuffs in stock colors only at no extra charge.

The prices printed in italics opposite items marked with ★ will be quoted only on orders for one half dozen or more. Quantity prices NOT allowed on items NOT marked with ★

Spalding Jacket Sweaters

Sizes 28 to 44 inch chest measurement. We allow four inches for stretch in all our sweaters, and sizes are marked accordingly. It is suggested, however, that for very heavy men a size about two inches larger than coat measurement be ordered to insure a comfortable fit.

No. VG. Showing special trimmed edging and cuffs supplied, if desired, on jacket sweaters at no extra charge.

BUTTON FRONT

No. **VG.** Best quality worsted, heavy weight, pearl buttons. Made in Gray, White and Dark Brown Mixture only.
Each, **$6.00** ★ *$60.00 Doz.*

No. **DJ.** Fine worsted, standard weight, pearl buttons, fine knit edging. Made in Gray, White and Sage Gray only.
Each, **$5.00** ★ *$54.00 Doz.*

No. **3J.** Standard weight wool, shaker knit, pearl buttons. In Gray or White only.
Each, **$4.50** ★ *$48.00 Doz.*

WITH POCKETS

No. **VGP.** Best quality worsted, heavy weight, pearl buttons. Made up in Gray or White only. With pocket on either side and a particularly convenient and popular style for golf players.
Each, **$6.50** ★ *$75.00 Doz.*

No. VGP

No. BG

Spalding Vest Collar Sweaters

No. **BG.** Best quality worsted, good weight. Gray or White only, with extreme open or low neck.
Each, **$5.50** ★ *$57.00 Doz.*

Boys' Jacket Sweater

No. **3JB.** This is an all wool jacket sweater, with pearl buttons; furnished in Gray only, and sizes from 30 to 36 inches chest measurement.
Each, **$3.00** ★ *$33.00 Doz.*

No. 3JB

SPECIAL NOTICE—We will furnish any of the above solid color sweaters with one color body and another color (not striped) collar and cuffs in stock colors only at no extra charge. This does not apply to the No. 3JB Boys' Sweater.

The prices printed in italics opposite items marked with ★ will be quoted only on orders for one half dozen or more. Quantity prices NOT allowed on items NOT marked with ★

Spalding Coat Jerseys

Following sizes carried in stock regularly in all qualities: 28 to 44 inch chest. Other sizes at an advanced price. We allow two inches for stretch in all our Jerseys, and sizes are marked accordingly. It is suggested, however, that for very heavy men a size about two inches larger than coat measurement be ordered to insure a comfortable fit. Any other combinations of colors or different width trimming or stripe to order only and at an advanced price. Quotations on application.

Nos. 10C and 12C

No. 10CP

The Spalding Coat Jerseys are made of the same worsted yarn from which we manufacture our better grade Jerseys, Nos. 10P and 12P, and no pains have been spared to turn them out in a well made and attractive manner. Colors: Solid Gray; Gray trimmed Navy; Gray trimmed Cardinal; Gray trimmed Dark Green. Pearl Buttons.

No. 10C. Same grade as our No. 10P. Each, **$3.50** ★ *$36.00 Doz.*

No. 12C. Same grade as our No. 12P. Each, **$3.00** ★ *$30.00 Doz.*

No. 10CP. Pockets, otherwise same as No. 10C. Each, **$4.00** ★ *$42.00 Doz.*

Spalding Striped and V-neck Jerseys

Nos. 10PW and 12PW

Nos. 10PX and 12PX

No. 12PV

No. 10PW. Good quality worsted, same grade as No. 10P. Solid color sleeves, 6-inch stripe around body. Colors: Black and Orange; Navy and White; Black and Red; Gray and Cardinal; Royal Blue and White; Columbia Blue and White; Scarlet and White; Navy and Cardinal; Maroon and White. Second color mentioned is for body stripe. Each, **$3.25** ★ *$33.00 Doz.*

No. 12PW. Worsted, with solid color sleeves and 6-in. stripe around body. Colors, same as No. 10PW. Each, **$2.75** ★ *$30.00 Doz.*

No. 10PX. Good quality worsted, fashioned; solid color body, with alternate striped sleeves, usually two inches of same color as body, with narrow stripe of any desired color. Colors same as No. 10PW. Each, **$3.25** ★ *$33.00 Doz.*

No. 12PV. Worsted, solid colors, has V-neck instead of full collar as on regular jerseys. Colors: Navy Blue, Black, Maroon and Gray. Ea., **$2.75** ★ *$30.00 Doz.*

No. 12PX. Worsted, solid color body, with alternate striped sleeves. Same arrangement and assortment of colors as No. 10PW. Each, **$2.75** ★ *$30.00 Doz.*

The prices printed in italics opposite items marked with ★ will be quoted only on orders for one-half dozen or more. Quantity prices NOT allowed on items NOT marked with ★

Spalding New and Improved Jerseys

Following sizes carried in stock regularly in all qualities:
28 to 44 inch chest. Other sizes at an advanced price.

Nos. 1P, 10P, 12P

We allow two inches for stretch in all our Jerseys, and sizes are marked accordingly. It is suggested, however, that for very heavy men a size about two inches larger than coat measurement be ordered to insure a comfortable fit.

No. 1P. Full regular made; that is, fashioned or knit to exact shape on the machine and then put together by hand, altogether different from cutting them out of a piece of material and sewing them on a machine as are the majority of garments known as Jerseys. Special quality worsted. Solid colors: Navy Blue, Black, Maroon and Gray.
Each, **$4.00** ★ *$42.00 Doz.*

No. 10P. Solid colors, worsted, fashioned. Colors: Navy Blue, Black, Maroon and Gray.
Each, **$3.00** ★ *$30.00 Doz.*

No. 12P. Worsted; colors as No 1P. . Each, **$2.50** ★ *$25.20 Doz.*

No. 12XB. Boys' Jersey. Worsted. Furnished in sizes 26 to 36 inches chest measurement only. Colors: Black, Navy Blue, Gray or Maroon; no special orders. . . . . Each, **$2.00** ★ *$21.00 Doz.*

No. 6. Cotton, good quality, fashioned, roll collar, full length sleeves. Colors: Black, Navy Blue, Gray and Maroon only. . Each, **$1.00**

No. 6X. Cotton, same as No. 6, but with striped sleeves in following combinations only: Navy with white or red stripe; Black with Orange or Red stripe; Maroon with White stripe. . . . Each, **$1.25**

Special Notice.— *We will furnish any of the above solid color Jerseys, except Nos. 6 and 6X, with one color body and another color (not striped) collar and cuffs in stock colors only at no extra charge.*

Woven Letters, Numerals or Designs.—We weave into our best grade Jerseys No. 1P, Letters, Numerals and Designs in special colors as desired. Prices quoted on application. Designs submitted.

The prices printed in italics opposite items marked with ★ will be quoted only on orders for one half dozen or more. Quantity prices NOT allowed on items NOT marked with ★

The Spalding Improved
Patent Ankle Supporter

Patented July 14, 1908—No. 892,064

Improved on original Hackey patent of which A. G. Spalding & Bros. were the sole licensees

There is no seam in the back of any of our ankle supporters. Nothing in their construction to chafe the foot, and they are shaped specially to fit back of foot snugly over heel. This is a patented feature.

Worn over or under stocking and support the ankle admirably, while not interfering in any way with free movements. Relieve pain immediately and cure a sprain in a remarkably short time. In ordering, give size of shoe worn

No. **H.** Soft tanned leather, best quality. . Pair, **$1.00**
No. **SH.** Good quality sheepskin, well made. " **.50**
No. **CH.** Black duck, lined and bound. . " **.25**

Knee Cap Bandage

In ordering, give circumference below knee, at knee and just above knee, and state if light or strong pressure is desired.
No. **4.** Cotton thread. Each, **$1.50**
No. **4A.** Silk thread. . " **2.00**

Elbow Bandage

In ordering, give circumference above and below elbow, and state if for light or strong pressure. **EACH**
No. **2.** Cotton thread. **$1.50**
No. **2A.** Silk thread. **2.00**

Spalding Wrist Bandage

Give circumference around smallest part of wrist, and state whether for light or strong pressure. **EACH**
No. **6.** Cotton thread. **$ .75**
No. **6A.** Silk thread. **1.00**

Ankle Bandage

In ordering, give circumference around ankle and over instep; state if light or strong pressure is desired. **EACH**
No. **5.** Cotton thread. **$1.50**
No. **5A.** Silk thread. **2.00**

Spalding Shoulder Cap Bandage

In ordering, give circumference around arm and chest. Mention for which shoulder required.

No. **1.** Cotton thread. Each, **$4.00**

No. **1A.** Silk thread. Each, **5.50**

Spalding Elastic Bandage

Composed of threads of rubber completely covered. Light, porous and easily applied. The pressure can be applied wherever necessary, following all depressions or swellings with folding and unvarying uniformity. Quickly secured by inserting end under last fold.
No. **30.** Width 3 inches, 5 yards long (stretched). . Each, **$1.00**
No. **25.** Width 2½ inches, 5 yards long (stretched). . Each, **75c.**

Spalding Elastic Belt

Our elastic foot ball belt stretches with the length of body and may be attached to jacket and pants, thus forming one continuous suit. By closely fitting the body, the opposing player has less chance of tackling. Allows perfect freedom in all positions.
No. **1.** Width 6 inch. Each, **$1.50**
This style belt is used in our No. VTJ Union Foot Ball Suit

Sandow's Patent
Spring Grip Dumb Bells

SANDOW PREPARING FOR HIS DAILY EXERCISE WITH HIS GRIP DUMB BELLS.

EUGEN SANDOW, Patentee.

A. G. SPALDING & BROS.

SOLE AMERICAN AND CANADIAN LICENSEES

AN ENTIRE SYSTEM of Physical Culture is embraced within the exercises possible with these wonderful dumb bells.

The bells are made in two halves connected by steel springs, the effort necessary in gripping compelling the pupil to continually devote his whole mind to each movement. This concentration of will power on each muscle involved is what is responsible for the great results obtained through properly exercising with them.

Sandow's Patent Spring Grip Dumb Bells

No. **6.** **MEN'S.** Nickel-plated; fitted with seven steel springs. . . . . Per pair, **$3.00**

No. **4.** **LADIES'.** Nickel-plated; fitted with five steel springs. . . . . Per pair, **$2.50**

No. **2.** **BOYS'.** Nickel-plated; fitted with four steel springs. . . . . Per pair, **$2.00**

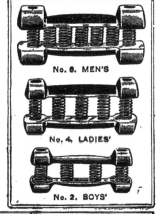

No. 6. MEN'S

No. 4. LADIES'

No. 2. BOYS'

We include with each pair of Sandow Dumb Bells a chart of exercises by Sandow and full instructions for using. Also a piece of selvyt cloth for keeping dumb bells in good condition.

Schoolyard Athletics

By J. E. SULLIVAN

President Amateur Athletic Union;
Member Board of Education Greater New York.

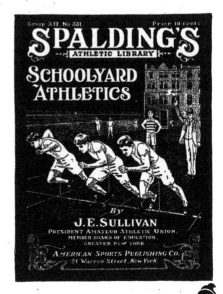

THE great interest in athletics that has developed in the public schools within recent years has led to the compilation of this book with a view to the systemization of the various events that form the distinctively athletic feature of school recreation. With its aid any teacher should be able to conduct a successful meet, while the directions given for becoming expert in the various lines will appeal to the pupil. Some of the leading athletes have contributed chapters on their specialties: Ray Ewry, holder of the world's high jump record, tells how to practice for that event; Harry Hillman, holder of the hurdle and three-legged records, gives hints on hurdle racing and three-legged racing; Martin Sheridan, all-around champion of America, gives directions for putting the shot; Harry F. Porter, high jump expert, describes how to become proficient in that event. The book is illustrated with photos taken especially for it in public school yards. **PRICE 10 CENTS**

Durand-Steel Lockers

Wooden lockers are objectionable, because they attract vermin, absorb odors, can be easily broken into, and are dangerous on account of fire.

Lockers made from wire mesh or expanded metal afford little security, as they can be easily entered with wire cutters. Clothes placed in them become covered with dust, and the lockers themselves present a poor appearance, resembling animal cages.

Durand-Steel Lockers are made of finest grade furniture steel and are finished with gloss black, furnace-baked japan (400°), comparable to that used on hospital ware, which will never flake off nor require refinishing, as do paints and enamels.

Some of the 6,000 Durand-Steel Lockers installed in Public Gymnasiums of Chicago. 12'x 15'x 42', Double Ti

Durand-Steel Lockers are usually built w doors perforated full length in panel design with si and backs solid. This prevents clothes in one loc from coming in contact with wet garme in adjoining lockers, while plenty of ver lation is secured by having the door per rated its entire length, but, if the purcha prefers, we perforate the backs also.

The cost of Durand-Steel Locke is no more than that of first-cla wooden lockers, and they last as lo as the building, are sanitary, secure, a in addition, are fire-proof.

THE FOLLOWING STANDARD SIZES AR THOSE MOST COMMONLY USED :

DOUBLE TIER	SINGLE TIER
12 x 12 x 36 inch	12 x 12 x 60 inch
15 x 15 x 36 inch	15 x 15 x 60 inch
12 x 12 x 42 inch	12 x 12 x 72 inch
15 x 15 x 42 inch	15 x 15 x 72 inch

SPECIAL SIZES MADE TO ORDER.

We are handling lockers as a special c tract business, and shipment will in eve case be made direct from the factory Chicago. If you will let us know the nu ber of lockers, size and arrangement, shall be glad to take up, through cor spondence, the matter of prices.

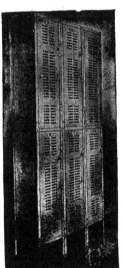

Six Lockers in Double Tier

Three Lockers in Single Tier

Communications addressed to **A. G. SPALDING & BROS.** in any of the following cities will receive attention.

For street numbers see inside front cover of this book

New York Syracuse Buffalo Pittsburg	Boston Philadelphia Baltimore	Washington Atlanta New Orleans	London England	Edinburgh Scotland	Montreal Canada	Chicago Cincinnati Cleveland	St. Louis Detroit Denver	San Francis Kansas Cit Minneapoli Seattle

Prices in effect January 5, 1909. Subject to change without notice.

Ankle Brace, Skate
Archery
Ash Bars
Athletic Library
Attachments, Chest Weight

Bags, Bathing Suit
Bags, Caddy
Bags, Cricket
Bags, Uniform
Balls, Base
Balls, Basket
Ball Cleaner, Golf
Balls, Cricket
Balls, Golf
Balls, Playground
Balls, Squash
Balls, Tennis
Bandages, Elastic
Bar Bells
Bar Stalls
Bars, Parallel
Bases, Base Ball
Bases, Indoor
Basket Ball Wear
Bathing Suits
Bats, Base Ball
Bats, Cricket
Bats, Indoor
Batting Cage, Base Ball
Belts
Bladders, Basket Ball
Bladders, Foot Ball
Bladders, Striking Bags
Blades, Fencing
Blouses, Umpire
Boxing Gloves

Caddy Badges
Caps, Base Ball
Caps, University
Caps, Skull
Center Forks, Iron
Center Straps, Canvas
Chest Weights
Coats, Base Ball
Collars, Swimming
Combination Uniforms
Corks, Running
Cricket Goods
Croquet Goods
Cross Bars

Discus, Olympic
Discs, Marking
Discs, Rubber Golf
Discs, Striking Bag
Dumb Bells

Emblems
Equestrian Pole
Exerciser, Home
Exhibition Clubs

Fencing Sticks
Field Hockey
Finger Protection
Flags, College
Flags, Marking
Foils, Fencing
Foot Balls, Association
Foot Balls, Rugby
Foot Ball Goal Nets
Foot Ball Timer
Foul Flags

Gloves, Base Ball
Gloves, Cricket
Gloves, Fencing
Gloves, Golf
Gloves, Handball
Gloves, Hockey
Glove Softener
Goals, Basket Ball
Goal Cage, Pole
Goals, Foot Ball
Goals, Hockey
Golf Clubs
Golf Counters
Golfette
Grips, Athletic
Grips, Golf
Guy Ropes and Pegs
Gymnasium, Home
Gymnasium Board, Home

Hammers, Athletic
Handballs
Handle Cover, Rubber
Hangers for Indian Clubs
Hats, University
Head Harness
Health Pull
Hob Nails
Hockey Sticks
Hole Cutter, Golf
Hole Rim, Golf
Horizontal Bars
Hurdles, Safety

Indoor Base Ball
Indian Clubs
Inflaters, Foot Ball
Inflaters, Striking Bag

Jackets, Fencing
Jackets, Foot Ball
Jackets, Swimming
Jerseys

Knee Protectors
Knickerbockers, Foot Ball

Lace, Foot Ball
Lanes for Sprints
Lawn Bowls
Leg Guards, Cricket
Leg Guards, Foot Ball
Leg Guards, Hockey
Leg Guards, Polo
Letters, Embroidered
Letters, Woven
Lockers, Durand-Steel

Mallet, Cricket
Markers, Tennis
Masks, Base Ball
Masks, Fencing
Masks, Nose
Masseur, Abdominal
Mattresses
Medicine Balls
Megaphones
Mitts, Base Ball
Mitts, Handball
Mitts, Striking Bag
Mocassins
Mouthpiece, Foot Ball

Needle, Lacing
Nets, Tennis
Net, Volley Ball
Numbers, Competitors

Pad, Chamois, Fencing
Pads, Foot Ball
Paint, Golf
Pants, Base Ball
Pants, Basket Ball
Pants, Boys' Knee
Pants, Foot Ball
Pants, Hockey
Pants, Roller Polo
Pants, Running
Pistol, Starter's
Plastrons, Fencing
Plates, Base Ball Shoe
Plates, Home
Plates, Marking
Plates, Pitchers' Box
Plates, Teeing
Platforms, Striking Bag
Poles, Ski
Poles, Vaulting
Polo, Roller, Goods
Protector, Abdomen
Protector, Elbow
Protector, Polo
Protection for Running Shoes
Pucks, Hockey
Push Ball
Pushers, Chamois
Puttees, Golf

Quantity Prices
Quoits

Racket Covers
Rackets, Lawn Tennis
Racket Presses
Rackets Restrung
Rapiers
Reels for Tennis Posts
Referees' Horns
Referees' Whistle
Rings, Exercising
Rings, Swinging
Rowing Machines
Roque

Scabbards for Skates
Score Board, Golf
Score Books, Base Ball
Score Books, Basket Ball
Score Books, Cricket
Score Books, Golf
Score Books, Tennis
Scoring Tablets, Base Ball
Seven-Foot Circle
Shin Guards, Association
Shin Guards, Rugby
Shin Guards, Hockey
Shin Guards, Polo
Shirts, Base Ball
Shirts, Basket Ball
Shirts, Sleeveless
Shoes, Base Ball
Shoes, Basket Ball
Shoes, Bowling
Shoes, Cross Country
Shoes, Cricket
Shoes, Fencing
Shoes, Foot Ball, Association
Shoes, Foot Ball, Rugby
Shoes, Golf
Shoes, Gymnasium
Shoes, Jumping
Shoes, Running

Shoes, Skating
Shoes, Squash
Shoes, Tennis
Shot, Indoor
Shot, Massage
Skate Bags
Skates, Hockey
Skate Holders
Skates, Ice
Skates, Racing
Skates, Rink, Ice
Skate Rollers
Skates, Roller
Skates, Tubular
Skate Straps
Skis
Sleeve Bands, College
Slippers, Bathing
Snow Shoes
Squash Goods
Standards, Vaulting
Standards, Volley Ball
Starters' Pistol
Steel Cable
Sticks, Polo
Stockings
Stop Boards
Striking Bags
Studs, Golf
Stumps and Bails
Suits, Union, Foot Ball
Supporters
Supporters, Ankle
Supporters, Wrist
Suspensories
Sweaters
Swimming Suits
Swivel Striking Bags
Swords, Fencing
Swords, Duelling

Tackling Machine
Take off Board
Tapes, Adhesive
Tapes, Marking
Tapes, Measuring
Tees, Golf
Tennis Posts
Tether Tennis
Tights
Toboggans
Toboggan Cushions
Toboggan Toe Caps
Toe Boards
Toques
Trapeze, Adjustable
Trapeze, Single
Trousers, Y. M. C. A.
Trunks, Bathing
Trunks, Velvet
Trunks, Worsted
Umpire Indicator
Uniforms, Base Ball
Varnish for Gut
Volley Balls
Water Polo Ball
Wands, Calisthenic
Watches, Stop
Water Wings
Weights, 56-lb.
Whistles, Referees'
Whitely Exerciser
Wrist Machine

When the season opens for the sale of such goods, with their misleading but alluring high list prices, the retailer begins to realize his responsibilities, and grapples with the situation as best he can, by offering "special discounts," which vary with local trade conditions.

Under this system of merchandising, the profits to both the manufacturer and the jobber are assured; but as there is no stability maintained in the prices to the consumer, the keen competition amongst the local dealers invariably leads to a demoralized cutting of prices by which the profits of the retailer are practically eliminated.

This demoralization always reacts on the manufacturer. The jobber insists on lower, and still lower, prices. The manufacturer. in his turn, meets this demand for the lowering of prices by the only way open to him, viz.: the cheapening and degrading of the quality of his product.

The foregoing conditions became so intolerable that, ten years ago, in 1899, A. G. Spalding & Bros. determined to rectify this demoralization in the Athletic Goods Trade, and inaugurated what has since become known as "The Spalding Policy."

The "Spalding Policy" eliminates the jobber entirely, so far as Spalding Goods are concerned, and the retail dealer secures his supply of Spalding Athletic Goods direct from the manufacturer under a restricted retail price arrangement by which the retail dealer is assured a fair, legitimate and certain profit on all Spalding Athletic Goods, and the consumer is assured a Standard Quality and is protected from imposition.

The "Spalding Policy" is decidedly for the interest and protection of the users of Athletic Goods, and acts in two ways:

> FIRST—The user is assured of genuine Official Standard Athletic Goods, and the same fixed prices to everybody.
>
> SECOND—As manufacturers, we can proceed with confidence in purchasing at the proper time, the very best raw materials required in the manufacture of our various goods, well ahead of their respective seasons, and this enables us to provide the necessary quantity and absolutely maintain the Spalding Standard of Quality.

All retail dealers handling Spalding Athletic Goods are required to supply consumers at our regular printed catalogue prices—neither more nor less—the same prices that similar goods are sold for in our New York, Chicago and other stores.

All Spalding dealers, as well as users of Spalding Athletic Goods, are treated exactly alike, and no special rebates or discriminations are allowed to anyone.

Positively, nobody; not even officers, managers, salesmen or other employes of A. G. Spalding & Bros., or any of their relatives or personal friends, can buy Spalding Athletic Goods at a discount from the regular catalogue prices.

This, briefly, is the "Spalding Policy," which has already been in successful operation for the past ten years, and will be indefinitely continued.

In other words, "The Spalding Policy" is a "square deal" for everybody.

A. G. SPALDING & BROS.

By *A. G. Spalding.*

PRESIDENT.

Standard Quality

An article that is universally given the appellation **"Standard"** is thereby conceded to be the Criterion, to which are compared all other things of a similar nature. For instance, the Gold Dollar of the United States is the Standard unit of currency, because it must legally contain a specific proportion of pure gold, and the fact of its being Genuine is **guaranteed** by the Government Stamp thereon. As a protection to the users of this currency against counterfeiting and other tricks, considerable money is expended in maintaining a Secret Service Bureau of Experts. Under the law, citizen manufacturers must depend to a great extent upon Trade-Marks and similar devices to protect themselves against counterfeit products—without the aid of "Government Detectives" or "Public Opinion" to assist them.

Consequently the "Consumer's Protection" against misrepresentation and "inferior quality" rests entirely upon the integrity and responsibility of the "Manufacturer."

A. G. Spalding & Bros. have, by their rigorous attention to "Quality," for thirty-three years, caused their Trade-Mark to become known throughout the world as a guarantee of Quality as dependable in their field as the U. S. Currency is in its field.

The necessity of upholding the guarantee of the Spalding Trade-Mark and maintaining the Standard Quality of their Athletic Goods, is, therefore, as obvious as is the necessity of the Government in maintaining a Standard Currency.

Thus each consumer is not only insuring himself but also protecting other consumers when he assists a Reliable Manufacturer in upholding his Trade-Mark and all that it stands for. Therefore, we urge all users of our Athletic Goods to assist us in maintaining the Spalding Standard of Excellence, by insisting that our Trade-Mark be plainly stamped on all athletic goods which they buy, because without this precaution our best efforts towards maintaining Standard Quality and preventing fraudulent substitution will be ineffectual.

Manufacturers of Standard Articles invariably suffer the reputation of being high-priced, and this sentiment is fostered and emphasized by makers of "inferior goods," with whom low prices are the main consideration.

A manufacturer of recognized Standard Goods, with a reputation to uphold and a guarantee to protect, must necessarily have higher prices than a manufacturer of cheap goods, whose idea of and basis for a claim for Standard Quality depends principally upon the eloquence of the salesman.

We know from experience that there is no quicksand more unstable than poverty in quality—and we avoid this quicksand by Standard Quality.

A. G. Spalding & Bros

Lightning Source UK Ltd.
Milton Keynes UK
UKHW02f0750090818
326991UK00010B/587/P